DROPSHIPPING

JONATHAN BECKER

TABLE OF CONTENTS

CHAPTER ONE

INTRODUCTION TO DROPSHIPPING

We are all aware of the business model where a retailer stocks the purchased items before he could sell it in the market, but the concept of dropshipping is quite a different one. A seller does not necessarily have to be the stock list of the items he sells. Everything can still happen in an organized manner. You might have thought, how all these can happen? Suppose you have a customer who wants to buy a product, but you do not own an inventory, neither do you stock up items. In that case, your product manufacturer or supplier directly delivers the product/s to your customer.

Now, this dropshipping mode has a number of advantages. Let us find out what they are:

Easy To Get Started

As you do not have to deal with physical products, this business is quite an easy one. If you are investing in the same you will not have to worry about packaging and shipping of the orders, renting or managing a warehouse, tracking inventory, maintaining stock levels by continuously ordering products, etc.

Requires Less Capital

This ecommerce business model requires a lot less to invest than retail businesses. One can launch an ecommerce store without having to risk his bank funds and property for a loan. All they need to do is purchase the product when a customer has already bought it by making a payment. So, without a major upfront inventory, it is possible to start a successful business.

Reduced Overheads

When there is no need to deal with inventory purchases our managing the same the overhead costs are sure to remain low. Studies have found that several successful dropshipping businesses are operated via a laptop from a remote location which can be the investor's home or office. The regular investment in many cases has been found to be lesser than $100. It may grow once there is growth in the business.

Wide Selection of Products

Under this model, one does not have to deal with a specific product but can earn from different products. You can add the items that a supplier stocks on your website at no additional charges.

Offers Flexibility over a Location

Any place that has uninterrupted internet connection can be used for a dropshipping business. Additionally, you will need to have a better hand at communicating with the suppliers and customers.

These are the reasons why dropshipping is considered to be an attractive model. If you are looking forward to increasing your income this can be one option you can look into.

Dropshipping! The Easy Way To Sell Hundreds Of Items On Ebay Without Ever Buying Or Holding Stock!

Imagine having top companies invent, design and buy products, test the market, employ world class copywriters to describe their products, hire top-notch graphic designers and photographers - and give you the whole lot FREE OF CHARGE! Well, that's exactly what you can do when you start using dropshipping as part of your eBay business.

Benefits of Dropshipping

1. Increase customers

Wholesale customers can display your products in their physical or online stores, and market your products directly to their line of customers. As online business owners, you will be able to indirectly expand your market and reach more customers; otherwise, you would not be able to have if you haven't partnered with wholesale buyers.

Dropshipping has a number of advantages namely reduced risk, lower capital, wide product selection, highly scalable and location independence.

2. Save on money, time and effort

Working with wholesale customers that already have a solid base of customers will save you a lot of time, money and effort.

Most people who are starting their first online business via auctions or online stores don't have a lot of money to buy a bunch of products or the space to warehouse and store the products they want to sell online. This is where working with a real Dropshipper will save you a ton of money. A real Dropshipper is simply a Certified Wholesaler who offers dropshipping. You find the Dropshipper you want to work with (the one who has the products you want to sell.) They will then give you access to their product images so that you can post them on your website, auction, blog or however you plan to sell online. When a customer orders the product, you then order the product from the Wholesaler and they ship it to your customer.

Merchants display your products in their online store and send you an invoice once a customer purchases your products. Once the orders are confirmed by the merchant, you ship the products from the warehouse to the address of the customer. In this order fulfillment process, both you and the wholesale buyer saved on the time to make a sale.

Wholesale merchants don't need to purchase stocks of inventory that might not be bought at all. With dropshipping, merchants order from store owners or manufacturers when customers already bought the product. It lessens the burden on merchants; at the same time, less effort for the store owners to find customers.

With eCommerce, dropshipping means less expenses for wholesale buyers since they only pay for products that are already sold. For the part of the manufacturers, it means more sales, product movement, and fulfilled orders. Partnering with reputable wholesale buyers who are also looking to increase their profits is a win-win situation for you. In this way, having more wholesale buyers will increase your sales and profits.

3. Increased Wholesale buyers

Wholesale buyers will be more likely to partner with you when you are a dropship wholesaler. Buyers do not need to a warehouse and stock inventories since you will be the one to ship the products directly to their customers.

Plus, wholesale buyers

On the other hand, Shopify wrote, "Running an e-commerce business is much easier when you don't have to deal with physical products. You don't have to manage a warehouse, pack, and ship orders, track inventory, handle returns, and manage product inventory."

4. Flexibility

The dropshipping model offers flexibility that would not be possible without it. Wholesale merchants can run the business anywhere and anytime as long as they have Internet connection. With the Internet, buyers can directly communicate with manufacturers or store owners at the same time with customers.

It gives flexibility to merchants since they can partner with multiple wholesale suppliers and sell more products to their customers. Manufacturers also get more flexibility since there is more product movement.

5. Leverage

In business, being able to multiply your money, time and effort is a form of leverage. By offering dropshipping to wholesale customers, you'll be able to prioritize on establishing relationships with these buyers.

Having reliable and dependable dropship wholesalers who will do the shipping for you balances the burden between the merchant and the supplier.

Other Advantages of Drop Shipping

The main advantage of drop shipping is that you do not have to stock or touch any product. When a customer orders a $100 pearl necklace from you and your supplier charges you $13, an invoice is sent to your supplier, they charge you $13, and they ship the pearl necklace to your customer. Meanwhile, you collect $100 for a profit of $87.

It is easy to get started

There is no need to manage, stock and organize inventories.

Assortment expansion

Easy to Scale up/Down

Allows you to function on a very low operating budget

Allows you to have a healthy cash flow, as you don't have to spend a lot until you start seeing money back

You don't need to have a website as you can sell at high-traffic marketplaces such as Amazon.com, eBay.com or other online marketplaces.

While average margins may be lower compared to other retail stores that stock their own inventory, there is no risk of a "bad buy" that results in over stock issues.

Disadvantages of Dropshipping

Although, there are also disadvantages to the dropshipping model. The disadvantages to dropshipping include errors in the product shipment, shipping problems, inventory issues, miscommunication, and low margins.

Aside from that, "You lose quality control since you can't see or use the product before it goes to the customer. You have take care of the return/complaint process yourself. You lose control over shipping quality or speed," according to E-commerce platforms.

Consider the advantages and disadvantages, and

whether this order fulfillment process will work for your business. If the pros outweigh the cons, then, it's time to start offering this service to your wholesale customers.

Drop shipping's ease of entry is a double-edged sword. As more merchants use it, drop shipping can become a rat race to the bottom. Here are the other disadvantages of drop shipping:

It is not easy to find a good, reliable drop shipper that does not serve thousands of other merchants.

You don't control anything except your prices and the products that you "offer".

Potential quality control issues

Risk in offering and selling products that are no longer available from the drop shipper supplier resulting in potential customer service issues

Reduced margins, or low profit margins especially if you find yourself competing with other online merchants that have set their shop's prices at rock bottom prices. With competitors making only minimal profits, if you try to match them or compete head on with their low prices you may find that your profits are only pennies.

Overcrowded market, with the dropshipper supplying the same products as you have to thousands of other drop ship sellers like you.

You may find yourself in a highly competitive drop shipping niche.

Does not guarantee profits.

Your store is only as good as your ecommerce platform.

Requires basic skills (at least) to manage an online store, including some technical knowledge like uploading products to shopping cart, cropping photos, writing unique product descriptions.

The more drop shipping suppliers you use, the more work you create for yourself.

Shipping costs charged by the drop shipper, which could vary across different drop shippers.

Paying shipping fees to your drop shipper while you are pressured to offer free shipping to your customer.

Drop shipper can make mistakes, as it is not a guarantee that they fulfill 100% of their orders 100% correctly.

If selling on huge marketplaces such as Amazon

(alongside thousands of other merchants using the same drop shipper), price comparison is easy and you may end up discounting and discounting just to beat everyone else.

Drop shipping is not an automatic path to success. In fact, it is hard work. It is not just setting a system that runs itself, orders come in, manufacturer ships and you pocket the difference. Since you may be just one of the merchant working with the same drop shipper and hustling for the same dollar, you need to make every effort to differentiate your business from the others.

Passive income, key to getting rich

One of the keys to getting rich and creating wealth is to understand the different ways in which income can be generated. It's often said that the lower and middle-class work for money whilst the rich have money work for them. The key to wealth creation lies within this simple statement.

Imagine, rather than you working for money that you instead made every dollar work for you 40hrs a week. Better still, imagine each and every dollar working for you 24/7 i.e. 168hrs/week. Figuring out the best ways you can make money work for you is an important step on the road to wealth creation.

In the US, the Internal Revenue Service (IRS) government agency responsible for tax collection and enforcement, categorizes income into three broad types: active (earned) income, passive income, and portfolio income. Any money you ever make (other than maybe winning the lottery or receiving an inheritance) will fall into one of these income categories. In order to understand how to become rich and create wealth it's vital that you know how to generate multiple streams of passive income.

Passive income is income generated from a trade or business, which does not require the earner to participate. It is often investment income (i.e. income that is not obtained through working) but not exclusively. The central tenet of this type of income is that it can expect to continue whether you continue working or not. As you near retirement you are most definitely seeking to replace earned income with passive, unearned income. The secret to wealth creation earlier on in life is passive income; positive cash-flow generated by assets that you control or own.

One of the reasons people find it difficult to make the leap from earned income to more passive sources of income is that the entire education system is actually pretty much designed to teach us to do a job and hence rely largely on earned income. This works for governments as this kind of income generates large volumes of tax but will not work for you if you're focus is on how to become rich and wealth building. However, to become rich and create wealth you will be required to cross the chasm from relying on earned income only.

The 3 Core Principles of a Passive Income Business

Let's talk about the basic building blocks that make up a passive income business. If you do any online searches for passive income businesses, you'll be drowning in links that tell you dozens of different approaches to what passive income is, and how to do it.

let's talk about the most basic building blocks that are necessary to have a passive income business.

In order to have a business, you need something to sell. The best way to do that is to have a product that you can sell. That's the first key ingredient to your passive income business.

A Great Product

It doesn't matter if the product is yours or an affiliate product. The product needs to be of high quality, and it really needs to solve a problem for your target market. If you don't already have a great product, concentrate on this element first. A great product that your market really wants and needs will be the single greatest asset in your passive income business.

Systems and Processes

Now that you've got a great product to sell, you need to setup the systems to sell it. In order to make this a passive activity, you need to set it up so you don't have to be present for the sales process to run. It needs to run completely on autopilot.

This is accomplished with a great foundation of sales and marketing systems. These systems should be comprehensive enough to operate independently of you. These systems can then generate detailed processes to become your passive income sales machine. The core processes you need initially is prospect attraction, sales, and product delivery. In other words, generating traffic, a sales funnel, and a product delivery system. These are also the main elements of your product website.

These systems and processes turn your product website (or affiliate website) into a lean mean selling machine.

Technology and Mobility

The final part of the puzzle is the technology necessary to make your systems and processes work. The good news is there are many very easy to use software packages that can make this a breeze. In fact, they take care of your systems and processes for you, without you even having to worry about the what and how of setting them up.

The last piece is the mobility and freedom this passive income business provides. Technology like smart phones and tablets allow you to keep an eye on these sales systems from anywhere. As long as you can get an Internet connection, you can run your business. Some of the more popular tables can even get you online from anywhere there is a cell phone signal.

CHAPTER TWO

TART DROPSHIPPING BUSINESS

How To Start A Dropshipping Business

If you're looking to start your own online business, but you just don't know where to start, look no further. There is no better time to start your own business and jump on one of the fastest growing trends in 2018 called "dropshipping". But "what is dropshipping" you may ask, dropshipping is a finding a supplier of a product and then reselling it on your website for a higher price. If you want to start your own dropshipping website, then Shopify is the right platform for you. The best part is you will never have to worry about physically owning the product(s) either! When you sell a product on your website,

you will purchase it from a third party vendor and the vendor will ship it directly to your customer on your behalf. Considering you are never seeing or handling the product, you are basically a middleman.

Here's a sample of how the entire ordering process might look:

Step 1 – Customer Places Order With Phone Outlet

Mr. Jason needs a case for his new smartphone and places an order via Phone Outlet's online store. Once the order is approved, a few things happen:

• Phone Outlet and Mr. Jason get an email confirmation (likely identical) of the new order that is automatically generated by the store software.

• Mr. Jason's payment is captured during the checkout process and will be automatically deposited into Phone Outlet's bank account.

Step 2 – Phone Accessory Outlet Places the Order With Its Supplier

This step is usually as simple as Phone Outlet forwarding the email order confirmation to a sales representative at Wholesale Accessories.

Phone Outlet's credit card on file and will bill it for the wholesale price of the goods, including any shipping or processing fees.

NOTE: Some sophisticated dropshippers will support automatic XML (a common format for inventory files) order uploading or the ability to place the order manually online, but email is the most common way to place orders with dropshipping suppliers because it's universal and easy to use.

Step 3 – Wholesale Accessories Ships the Order

Assuming the item is in stock and the wholesaler was able to successfully charge Phone Outlet's card,

Wholesale Accessories will box up the order and ship it directly to the customer. Though the shipment comes from Wholesale Accessories, Phone Outlet's name and address will appear on the return address label and its logo will appear on the invoice and packing slip. Once the shipment has been finalized, Wholesale Accessories will email an invoice and a tracking number to Phone Outlet.

NOTE: The turnaround time on dropshipped orders is often faster than you'd think. Most quality suppliers will be able to get an order out the door in a few hours, allowing merchants to advertise same-day shipping even when they are using a dropshipping supplier.

Step 4 – Phone Outlet Alerts the Customer of Shipment

Once the tracking number is received, Phone Outlet will send the tracking information to the customer, likely using an email interface that's built in to the online store interface. With the order shipped, the payment collected and the customer notified, the order and fulfillment process is complete. Phone Outlet's profit (or loss) is the difference between what it charged Mr. Jason and what it paid Wholesale Accessories.

Dropshippers Are Invisible

Despite its critical role in the ordering and fulfillment process, the dropshipper is completely invisible to the end customer. When the package is received, only Phone Outlet's return address and logo will be on the shipment. If Mr. Jason's receives the wrong case, he would contact Phone Outlet, which would then coordinate behind the scenes with Wholesale Accessories to get the right item sent out.

The dropshipping wholesaler doesn't exist to the end customer. Its sole responsibility is to stock and ship products. Everything else – marketing, website development, customer service, etc. – is the responsibility of the merchant. Before searching for suppliers, it's critical to know how to differentiate between legitimate wholesale suppliers and retail stores posing as wholesale suppliers. A true wholesaler buys directly from the manufacturer and will usually be able to offer you significantly better pricing.

How Much Do Dropshippers Make?

So how much do dropshippers make? I was curious as well to see what other people were making and it certainly didn't disappoint. Based off a few Google searches I saw some people are making a fortune. Some dropshippers are making $800 a day and some are even making millions a year just from dropshipping someone else's product. I read a story about a guy who makes $3 million a year dropshipping cat shirts; yes shirts with cats on them made him rich. These people are doing it and who knows you could be next. Maybe you won't make a million dollars from this but an extra $100 a week could go a long way.

How To Become A Dropshipper

Here is a quick list of all the websites and information you will need to start your dropshipping business. These are my recommendations you are entitled to run your business as you wish. I will go into detail later on in the book, but this was to highlight the main speaking points. You can start a dropshipping business with just a Shopify account, the other tools and websites are just options for you.

· Join Shopify, for just $29.95 a month you can have your own online store. Shopify is the platform that you will be hosting your website on and adding your products to. There are other platforms but in my opinion Shopify is the easiest to use and is the most user friendly for a dropshipping business. (All you need to start).

· Register your business. I recommend you form a legitimate business to protect your assets but this is up to you. You can do this all online at My Company Works. This is strongly recommended but many dropshippers do not do this.

· Sign up for a business credit card, you will be making a lot of purchases for your products. Rather than using your personal credit card you should have a professional business credit card.

· I also recommend joining AliExpress this is a good site to buy your products to dropship.

· Sign up for the Burner App. This is a paid app on your phone that will give you a second phone number on your phone. For $4.99 a month you can receive calls and texts from potential customers without giving them your personal number.

· Rent a PO Box with a real address you can use the online service ipostal1.com and register online or you can go to your local UPS Store and get your own PO

Box. You can use the real street address as your business address.

· Join Fiverr, this website is great because for $5 you can get people to write your content for you or even provide SEO services, such as building backlinks to your website. Make sure you read the reviews about the person you are thinking about using.

How To Start A Dropshipping Business On Shopify

In this section I will talk about how to setup your Shopify dropshipping website, how to file for a business, and all the necessary steps you will need to set up your business.

I'm going to walk you through the steps of creating your own Shopify website; however, I will keep it super high level. Once you sign up to Shopify feel free to search on YouTube and see how other people created their account.

How To Build A Shopify Store For Your Dropshipping Business

1. Sign Up With Shopify: To create your account go to Shopify.com and enter your email address, password, and store name. Your store name will have to be unique (no one else has the store name yet) or Shopify will not let you create a store. When you join

using this link you will get a 14 day free trial with no obligations. If you are serious about starting a dropshipping business I would recommend starting out with a "Basic Shopify" account which is under $30 a month. If you're seeing success with your Shopify website you can always upgrade to a better plan the next month, but be patient you may not see great results until at least 6 months.

2. Set Up Your Online Store: After you've signed up you'll be directed to your account dashboard. You can start customizing your store's theme, upload products, set up payment options, set up your shipping rates, and buy a web domain. You can buy a domain from Shopify for about $14 a year. Now there are cheaper ways to buy a domain such as GoDaddy, however you'll have to redirect the DNS records yourself. To be honest I have no clue what that is or how hard it is to learn. Personally I would buy a domain name from Shopify, but if money is tight you can buy a domain on GoDaddy for $.99 with a promo code and then just Google about how to redirect the DNS records.

3. Choose A Theme: Make sure you choose a theme that you like and that makes sense for the products you sell. There are a lot of free themes/layouts available on Shopify but to have a unique look to your

website you many want to think about purchasing a theme. When purchasing a theme keep in mind it is a one-time purchase so once you buy it, it's yours for as long as you keep your website going. Themes can range in price but the most I've seen was $180, but they look awesome! Keep in mind the appearance of your website will help with your conversions.

4. Add Your Products: On the left side navigator there is a tab called "products" you'll want to click this and the click on "add a product" to populate your merchandise. For each product you will want to give it a good name, a detailed description, and a custom URL or "slug". This is a good way to work on optimizing your products for search engines (SEO). A slug is no more than adding a keyword at the end of your websites URL. You will also want to have a high quality picture of each product. Once all the information looks good hit the "save product" button on the top and bottom right corners.

5. Set Up Your Payment Options: One of the most important parts is to set up your payment options. It would be in your best interest to accept all major credit cards and PayPal as payment this way you won't lose out on sales if a customer only has one credit card or only PayPal. Keep in mind that each payment gateway has fees involved, so take these

fees into consideration when setting your prices. If you have the "Basic Shopify" package there is a set fee for credit card orders of 2.9% of the sale + $.30 per sale, the middle plan called "Shopify" charges 2.6% +$.30 per sale, and the "Advanced Shopify" charges 2.4% +$.30. So selling low margin items might be difficult. If you use any one of the dropshipping example products I provided above you should be profitable regardless of the credit card fees.

6. Get Your Site Live: Before you go live you'll want to go to the "General" tab and fill out your company's information. I would also recommend you add Google Analytics to your Shopify account to track users coming to your website and other helpful data. Make sure you fill in the tax information if you plan on collecting taxes as you should. Also make sure to fill out the shipping information even though your supplier should be shipping the product directly to your customer for free. You'll want to tell everyone who goes to your website what the shipping windows are and possibly even offer them a faster shipping method. You can even make money of this option, if you offer express shipping to get the product sooner and say it will cost you $2 extra to do this charge your customer $3 that way you make an extra dollar profit. The shipping windows are pretty long, but that is expected since it's free shipping and most likely the

product is coming from overseas. Once all that's done push your site live!

That's all it takes to creating your website on Shopify. In just a half an hour to an hour you can have a great looking website up and running without being an expert in web developing. Shopify makes it easy and with so many free resources available online you can find the answer to anything if you find yourself stuck on some aspect of the site. If you want to become a dropshipper I highly recommend you look into Shopify for all your website needs.

Dropshipping on eBay

As the world's largest auction site for physical goods online, eBay is a site most people know well. The following are some reasons you might want to consider – or avoid – dropshipping on eBay:

The Advantages of Selling on eBay

EASY TO GET STARTED – With eBay you can immediately dive in and start listing your wholesale products. Create an account, add a listing and you're in business.

ACCESS TO A LARGE AUDIENCE – When you list on eBay, you have access to the many online buyers who frequent the auction giant. Millions of people will see your listings, and the fairly robust and active market will help ensure you get a decent price for your products.

LESS MARKETING – Because you're able to piggyback off eBay's enormous platform, you don't need to worry about marketing, SEO or paying for traffic. This saves you time, as marketing is one of the biggest challenges associated with launching a dropshipping business.

Evaluating Sales Channels.

The Disadvantages of Selling on eBay

LISTING FEES – The biggest downside to eBay are the fees you'll have to pay 25. The most notable is the success fee, which can be up to 10% – or higher – of the sale prices of your items. In the dropshipping market, where margins are already fairly thin, this will cut into a large portion of your profits.

CONSTANT MONITORING AND RE-LISTING – eBay is an auction-style marketplace, so you'll need to be constantly monitoring and re-listing the products you want to sell. Some tools help automate this process, but it's still not as straightforward as listing a static product for sale on your own ecommerce website.

CAN'T CUSTOMIZE YOUR SALES PLATFORM – Your

product listings need to follow eBay templates, making it more difficult to create a professional, value adding page for your items.

NO LONG-TERM CONNECTION WITH CUSTOMERS – You might have a few repeat eBay customers, but most will probably never buy from you again. Any goodwill you bank up through excellent service will likely be lost.

The marketplace structure is created to serve itself. eBay doesn't want to focus on the merchants (you), they only want to focus on the products. You will be significantly restricted in how you communicate with customers, how you brand yourself, the design of your store, and so on.

YOU'RE NOT BUILDING AN ASSET – When you create a store that generates traffic and has repeat customers, you're building a real business with value that you can sell to someone else. When you sell on eBay, you're not building a lasting brand or web property with any tangible value that can be sold in the future.

Dropshipping on Amazon

Although Amazon stocks and sells a number of items, many of the products listed are actually sold by third-party merchants via Amazon's website. Like eBay, Amazon acts to help facilitate the sale and to resolve any problems that arise.

The Advantages of Selling on Amazon

The advantages of selling on Amazon are similar to the ones discussed for eBay: it's easy to get started, you have immediate access to a large audience and you don't need to worry about marketing or SEO.

Amazon also offers its own fulfillment warehouses (Fulfillment by Amazon), which allow you to complement your drop shipped items with products of your own without having to deal with packing, shipping or warehousing.

The Disadvantages of Selling on Amazon

LISTING FEES – As with eBay, you pay for access to this large network of buyers through fairly substantial commission fees. Amazon's commission fees vary by product type but are usually in the 10% to 15% range. Again, if you're working with relatively small dropshipping margins, this will take a hefty chunk out of your profits.

EXPOSURE OF SALES DATA – One risk you take using Amazon's platform is that Amazon can see all of your sales data, from the items that sell best to how much you're selling overall. Amazon has been accused of using this data to identify great selling opportunities and strengthen its own involvement in the niche, ultimately pushing out other merchants selling through its marketplace.

NO LONG-TERM CONNECTION WITH CUSTOMERS – Same deal as eBay, it's unlikely that you'll be able to grow a long-term relationship with your customers. Amazon exists to help themselves, so it's in there best interest to focus on the products and not the sellers. Be prepared to be severely restricted on how you can brand your business, display your products and communicate with your customers.

NO CUSTOMIZATION – Again like eBay you're going to be really limited in terms of customization. Everything you do in terms of branding, UI, marketing, and everything else is under Amazon's control.

Dropshipping With Your Own Online Store

The alternative to selling through third-party sites like Amazon and eBay is establishing your own online store to sell products. This is the method that attracts most people interested in building a successful dropshipping business.

The Advantages of Selling on Your Own Store

MORE CONTROL – With your own online store you get to create a shopping environment that's conductive to selling your products and most importantly adding value to your customers. You can customize the look and layout, and create custom product pages optimized to best inform your customers about the products.

EASY DESIGN – Building your own ecommerce store is easy, especially with platforms like Shopify. Simply choose a store design out of hundreds of options, make any customizations you want, add your products, hook up a payment gateway and you're up and running. Depending on the type of online store you're looking to create, you can be up and running in one day.

MOBILE READY – Selling on eBay and Amazon via mobile can be a pain. If you choose to build your online store with well respected hosted ecommerce platform your site will likely be responsive, which means it will look great on an iPad or mobile phone. This is increasingly important these days, as nearly 30% of online purchases are made via a mobile device.

Some online store platforms, like Shopify, let you

manage your entire business from your mobile device. This is particularly attractive to dropshipping business owners who often like to run their business on-the-go, or even on the beach somewhere.

NO THIRD-PARTY FEES – You won't have to pay 10% to 15% of every sale to eBay or Amazon, which will significantly improve your profit margins. All-in-all you're going to make more money by setting your dropshipping business up with an online store.

BUILDING A REAL BUSINESS – You're able to build a long-term business with a distinctive feel, known expertise and repeat customers. Most importantly, you'll be building a business with equity. It's much easier to sell a business built around an independently owned website.

The Disadvantages of Selling on Your Own Store

LESS FREE TRAFFIC – With your own site, you'll be responsible for generating traffic through marketing, SEO and paid advertising. There's more cost involved either money or time invested and you'll need to be willing to invest in a long-term campaign to promote your new store.

INCREASED COMPLEXITY – On Amazon and eBay, you don't have to think too much; simply fill out the standard template and publish your product listing. With your own site, you're ultimately responsible for configuring the design, layout and structure of your store. And if you're hosting your own store (versus using a hosted service like Shopify), you'll be responsible for any technical configuration related to the software and servers.

Which Sales Strategy Should You Choose?

So which platform should you choose? There's a lot to consider, and different platforms will be better suited for different people and situations. If you're looking to dip your toes into the dropshipping waters and explore it as a hobby, selling on eBay and Amazon can be a viable way to move forward if you can find products with enough margin to cover your fees and still make a profit.

There are many people making money selling on eBay and Amazon so you shouldn't dismiss it. But if you're serious about building a long-term business, i recommend starting your own ecommerce store. As discussed above, it offers the most flexibility, customization, ability to connect with customers, the chance to build real brand equity, and so much more. You'll need to invest in marketing and promotion, especially in the early days, but I think it offers the best long-term potential and is truly the only option for those serious about selling online.

Also, there's nothing wrong with selling a few items on eBay and Amazon while you're in the early stages of building your store. In fact, a number of mature, established brands sell merchandise this way, particularly through Amazon.

If you've never run a dropshipping business, the information in this chapter could

save you weeks of wasted time and frustration. Many of these detailed suggestions are drawn from two basic principles about dropshipping:

1. ACCEPT THAT THINGS CAN GET MESSY – The convenience of dropshipping comes at a price, and having an invisible third party involved in each sale often complicates things. From botched orders to out-of-stock items, fulfillment problems will be something you'll have to deal with. If you accept this ahead of time, you're less likely to throw in the towel due to frustration.

2. ADOPT A KISS MENTALITY – Having a KISS (Keep It Simple, Stupid!) mentality will serve you well with the dropshipping model. Given the inherent complexity of dropshipping multiple suppliers, shipments from various locations, etc. it's easy to think you need to

set your system to perfectly track your costs and inventory at all times. But if you try to do this, you'll likely go crazy, spend thousands on custom development and never launch a store. Focusing on the easiest-to-implement solutions, even if they're not "perfect," is usually the better option – especially when you're starting out.

With these two concepts in mind, let's discuss how to structure your business operationally to make things run as smoothly as possible.

When Suppliers Botch an Order

Even great suppliers make mistakes, and you're guaranteed to have fulfillment errors from time to time. So what do you do when your supplier sends the wrong item – or nothing at all?

Running a Dropshipping Company

OWN THE MISTAKE – Under no circumstances should you blame your dropshipper for the mistake. It will only cause confusion and make you look like an amateur. The customer has no idea the drop shipper even exists. Instead, you need to own the problem, apologize and let the customer know what you're doing to fix it.

MAKE IT UP TO THEM – Depending on the level of the

mistake, you may want to proactively offer the customer something for the error. This could mean refunding the shipping fee or an upgrade if the customer needs a new item shipped out.

MAKE THE SUPPLIER PAY TO FIX IT – You may have to assume responsibility for the error, but that doesn't mean you need to pay for it! Any reputable supplier will pay to fix its own errors, including paying for shipping costs to return items.

However, it probably won't pay for any freebies or upgrades you gave the customer (see above). You need to chalk those up as public relations and brand building expenses. Again, even the best suppliers will occasionally make mistakes, but be extremely wary of a supplier that habitually botches your orders and fails to fulfill them properly. Unless you can get the supplier to change (unlikely), your business's reputation will suffer. If this is the case, you should probably start looking for another supplier.

Managing Inventory & Multiple Suppliers

Most experienced dropshippers would agree that managing the status of inventory across multiple suppliers is the biggest challenge you'll face running a dropshipping business. Do a poor job of this and you'll be constantly informing customers that their order is out of stock – not a great way to attract repeat business and loyal brand fans.

Properly managing inventory across your suppliers – and limiting the number of out-of-stock items you sell – is a complex process. Web-based services, like Ordoro and eCommHub can help you sync inventory. This is a great option when suppliers offer real-time data feeds, but suppliers don't always have them.

Below are some best practices for inventory management that should help drastically reduce the number of out-of-stock items you sell:

1. USE MULTIPLE SUPPLIERS – Having access to multiple suppliers can be a huge advantage. Why? Because having multiple suppliers with overlapping inventory is the BEST way to improve your order fulfillment ratio. If supplier A doesn't have an item in stock, there's a good chance supplier B has it. Additionally, it's risky to rely on one supplier as the only place to source your product. If they decide not to work with you, raise their prices or go out of business it jeopardizes the future of your business. You'll never be able to find two suppliers that carry all the same products, but if they operate in the same niche or industry, both will likely stock the best-selling items – and these are what you're most concerned about.

2. PICK YOUR PRODUCTS WISELY – Drawing on the last point, try to sell primarily items that you know are carried by both suppliers. This way, you have two potential fulfillment options.

3. USE GENERICS TO YOUR ADVANTAGE – Even if they don't have exactly the same item, two suppliers might carry near-identical products that are interchangeable. This is particularly true for smaller accessories and product add-ons. If you can confirm that two products are nearly identical, write a generic product description that allows you to fulfill the order from either supplier. Also, list both suppliers' model numbers in the model field. That way you can forward an order invoice to either supplier without having to make changes.

A word of warning: You need to exercise some judgment in this area. Each market will have well-known brands (e.g., Nike, Bose), and you should NEVER substitute those products.

4. CHECK ON ITEM AVAILABILITY – Just because a dropshipper lists an item on its website doesn't mean it carries that item consistently. It's a good idea to chat with your sales representative about the availability of products you're considering selling. Are these items in stock 90% of the time or more? Or does the dropshipper keep only a few on hand and

often has trouble getting the product reordered from the manufacturer? You'll want to avoid stocking the latter type of products.

5. DEALING WITH OUT-OF-STOCK ORDERS - Despite your best planning, you'll inevitably deal with customer orders you can't fill. Instead of telling the customer the item is out of stock, offer a complimentary upgrade to a similar but better product. Your customer will likely be thrilled, and you'll be able to retain the customer relationship. You might not make any money on the order, and that's OK. You wouldn't have made any money had your customer canceled the order, either.

Order Fulfillment

Utilizing multiple suppliers has a number of benefits that we've discussed: it increases the likelihood that items will be in stock, offers geographical diversity for faster delivery times and prevents you from being reliant on any one source for your products. But with multiple options for filling an order, how do you know which supplier to choose? There are a few different methods to consider:

ROUTE ALL ORDERS TO A PREFERRED SUPPLIER – If you have one supplier that's best to work with (superior service, great selection, etc.), you can simply route all orders to that supplier by default. This is particularly easy to implement, as you can simply add your supplier's email address as a recipient for all new order confirmations, automating the entire process. If you use this method, ideally your preferred supplier will stock most of the items you sell. Otherwise, you'll frequently have to deal with re-routing orders that it couldn't fill.

ROUTE ORDERS BASED ON LOCATION – If you use multiple suppliers that each stock the majority of your products, you can simply route the order to the supplier closest to your customer. This not only expedites delivery to your customer, but also saves on shipping fees.

ROUTE ORDERS BASED ON AVAILABILITY – If you stock a large catalog of products spread out over numerous suppliers, you'll likely need to route each order based on which drop shipper has the item in stock. This option requires more work if you're doing it manually but can be automated with a service like eCommHub if your suppliers provide data feeds.

ROUTE ORDERS BASED ON PRICE – This sounds great in theory, but unless one supplier has significantly better pricing it can be difficult to automatically determine which supplier will be cheapest. Any automated solution will need to consider potential drop fees, real-time shipping rates and real-time supplier pricing. So while not impossible, it can be difficult to implement an accurate automated system to accomplish this.

NOTE: Even if you don't route all your orders on price, you should have your suppliers bid against each other to achieve the best pricing possible as your business grows. Just don't try to do this too early – if you're asking for pricing discounts as a newbie, you'll likely only annoy your suppliers. I 've tried all four methods and found there's no "best" way to do it. It really depends on your store, your suppliers and your personal preferences.

Security and Fraud Issues

Storing Credit Card Numbers

Storing your customers' credit card information can allow for convenient reordering and may increase sales. But if you're hosting your own site, this typically isn't worth the security issues and liability. To store credit card data you'll need to abide by all sorts of PCI (Payment Card Industry) compliance rules and security audits. This process is expensive and complex, especially for nontechnical merchants. And if your server is hacked or breached, you might be liable for the stolen card information. The best solution is to not store your customers' credit card data. Focus your efforts on marketing and customer service instead of security audits. Fortunately, if you're using a hosted platform like Shopify you won't need to worry about any of this. But if you're using a self-hosted cart, make sure to disable the "store card information" feature in your configuration panel.

Dealing With Fraudulent Orders

The possibility of fraudulent orders can be scary when you're starting out, but with some common sense and a bit of caution you can prevent the vast majority of losses due to fraud.

The Address Verification System

The most common and widely used fraud prevention measure is the AVS, or address verification system. When the AVS feature is enabled, customers must enter the address on file with their credit card for the transaction to be approved. This helps prevent thieves with just the raw credit card number from successfully making purchases online. Fraud is rare for orders that pass the AVS check and are shipped to the customers' billing addresses. The vast majority of fraudulent ecommerce orders occur when the billing and shipping addresses are different. In these cases, a thief enters the card owner's address as the billing address and enters a separate shipping address for the goods. Unfortunately, if you don't allow customers to ship to addresses other than the billing address, you'll lose out on a lot of legitimate orders. But by allowing it, you're at risk for fraudulent orders that YOU will have to pay for. If you ship an order to an address other than the card holder's address, the credit card company will make you foot the bill in the event of fraud. Fortunately, fraudsters tend to follow patterns that make it easier to spot illegitimate orders before they ship. Individually, these signs won't help you flag a fraudulent order, but if you see two or three of them you should investigate:

• DIFFERENT BILLING AND SHIPPING – Again, more than 95% of all fraudulent orders will have different billing and shipping addresses.

• DIFFERENT NAMES – Different names on the billing and shipping addresses could be a red flag for fraudulent orders. That, or a gift purchase.

• UNUSUAL EMAIL ADDRESSES – Most people have email addresses incorporating some part of their name, allowing you to match part of an email address to a customer's name. But if you see an address like dfssdfsdf@gmail.com, there's a good chance it's a made-up address and is one sign of fraud.

• EXPEDITED SHIPPING — Since they're charging everything to someone else's card, fraudsters will often pick the fastest and most expensive delivery method. It also reduces the amount of time you have to catch them before the item is delivered.

If you spot an order you suspect is fraudulent, simply pick up the phone.

Fraudsters almost never put their real number on an order. If the order is legitimate, you'll likely have a 30-second discussion with someone that clears everything up. If not, you'll get a dead number or someone who has no idea that she ordered a 25-foot boat scheduled for overnight delivery. At that point, you can cancel the order and issue a refund to avoid any chargebacks or problems.

Understanding Chargebacks

When a customer calls his or her bank or credit card company to contest a charge made by you, you'll receive what's called a "chargeback." Your payment processor will temporarily deduct the amount of the disputed charge from your account and ask you to prove that you delivered the goods or services to the customer. If you can't provide proof, you'll lose the amount in question and be slapped with a $25 chargeback processing fee. If you rack up too many chargebacks relative to the volume of orders you're processing, you could even lose your merchant account.

The largest cause of chargebacks is usually fraud, but customers will also dispute a charge because they didn't recognize your business, forgot about the transaction or simply didn't like the product they received. We've seen it all.

When you receive a chargeback, you often have just a few days to respond, so you need to act quickly! To have a shot at getting your money back, you'll need to provide documentation of the original order, tracking information showing delivery and likely a wholesale packing slip showing which items you purchased and shipped. If the contested charge was for a legitimate transaction, you'll have a good chance of recovering the funds as long as you didn't make any untrue statements or promises in the course of the transaction.

Unfortunately, if the chargeback is related to an order with different billing and shipping addresses, you're almost certainly not going to win. Most processors will only compensate you for fraudulent orders shipped to the billing address on the card. In our businesses, we don't even bother responding to these kind of chargebacks because we know it's a waste of time.

Dealing With Returns

Before writing your own return policy, you'll want to make sure you know and understand how all your suppliers deal with returns. If they have a lax 45-day return window, you can afford to be generous with your terms. A strict return policy from just one supplier can cause you to re-evaluate the terms you can afford to have in place. When a customer needs to return an item, the process will look like this:

1. A customer contacts you to request a return

2. You request an RMA (return merchandise authorization) number from your supplier

3. The customer mails back the merchandise to your supplier, noting the RMA on the address

4. The supplier refunds your account for the wholesale price of the merchandise

5. You refund the customer for the full price of the merchandise It's not always this straightforward, however. The following can complicate returns:

Restocking Fees

Some suppliers will charge a restocking fee, which is essentially a surcharge for having to return an item. Even if your supplier charges these fees, we strongly recommend not having them be a part of your return policy. They seem outdated and unfriendly toward customers. Although you may have to eat a fee here and there, you'll likely recoup that expense in more customers who decide to do business with you.

Defective Items

The only thing worse than receiving a defective item is having to pay additional postage to return it! Most dropshipping suppliers won't cover return postage for defective items. In their minds, they didn't manufacture the item so they aren't liable for defects. They simply view it as a risk of selling products to a retail market.

You, however, should ALWAYS compensate your customers for the return shipping fees for defective items if you're interested in building a reputable business. Again, this is a fee you won't be able to pass along to anyone, but it's part of the cost of running a quality dropshipping business. Unless you have your own UPS or FedEx account, it can be difficult to print a pre-paid shipping label for customers so you may need to issue a return shipping refund to compensate them for their out-of-pocket expense. However you do it, make sure you compensate them somehow. If the defective item is relatively inexpensive, it often makes sense to just ship the customer a new product without requiring them to return the old one. This has a number of advantages compared to making them return the old item, including:

IT CAN BE COST EFFECTIVE – It doesn't make sense to pay $10 to return an item that only costs you $12 from your wholesaler. You'll get a $2 net credit, but it's not worth it for the hassle to your customer, supplier and staff.

THE CUSTOMER IS BLOWN AWAY – How often do companies simply ship out a new product without needing an old one back? Almost never! You'll score major points and may land a customer for life. Also, the customer will get the new product much faster than if the old one had to be returned to the warehouse before the new item could be shipped.

YOUR SUPPLIER MAY PAY FOR SHIPPING – Suppliers won't pay for return on a defective product, but most will pay to have a new replacement sent to the customer. Because they'll be paying for return shipping anyway, most suppliers can be talked into covering the shipping on a replacement product that you simply purchase separately. Plus, many are glad to duck the hassle of processing the return. If a customer wants to return a non-defective product for a refund, most companies will expect the buyer to pay for the return freight. This is a fairly reasonable policy. If you're willing to offer free returns on everything, you'll definitely stand out (and companies like Zappos have made this part of their unique business model). But it can get expensive, and most customers will understand that you shouldn't have to cough up return shipping fees simply because they ordered a product they ultimately didn't want.

Shipping Issues

Calculating shipping rates can be a big mess for dropshipping merchants. With so many different products shipping from multiple locations, it's difficult to accurately calculate shipping rates for orders. There are three types of shipping rates you can use:

REAL-TIME RATES – With this method, your shopping cart will use the collective weight of all items purchased and the shipping destination to get an actual real time quote. This is very accurate but can be difficult to compute for shipments from multiple warehouses.

PER-TYPE RATES – Using a per-type method, you'll set flat shipping rates based on the types of products ordered. So all small widgets would ship for a flat $5 rate, while all large widgets would be $10 to ship.

FLAT-RATE SHIPPING – As the name implies, you'd

charge one flat rate for all shipments, regardless of type. You could even offer free shipping on all orders.

This method is the easiest to implement but is the least accurate in reflecting actual shipping costs.

When it comes to shipping, it's important to refer to the overarching principles about dropshipping that we listed at the outset of this chapter. Specifically, we want to find a solution that emphasizes simplicity over perfection, especially if we're just starting out.

Some merchants will spend days or weeks struggling to properly configure automated shipping rules for a store that has yet to generate a sale. Instead, they should focus on other issues like marketing and customer service, and quickly implement a shipping policy that makes sense from an overall level.

Then, once they start to grow, they can invest in a more exact system. With this philosophy, it's often best to estimate an average shipping fee and set that as your overall flat rate. You'll probably lose money on some orders but make it back on others.

Even if you could implement a system that passed along extra shipping fees based on supplier location, would you really want to? Most customers balk at excessive shipping fees, especially when they assume their order is originating from one location. Instead, try to limit multiple shipments by using suppliers with overlapping inventory and by being selective about the items you sell. This is a much more practical and simple long-term solution.

International Shipments

International shipping has become easier but it's still not as straightforward as domestic shipping. When you ship internationally, you'll need to consider and/or deal with:

• Different weight and length limitations for different countries

• Additional charges from suppliers for processing international orders

• The added expense of resolving problematic orders due to higher shipping fees

• Excessive costs for shipping large and/or heavy items Is the hassle worth it? It depends on the market you're in and the margins you earn. If you sell small items with higher margins, the increased market reach may make it worthwhile to deal with the hassle and expense of offering international shipments. For others especially merchants selling larger or heavier items the added benefit won't be worth the expense and inconvenience.

Picking a Carrier

Selecting the right carrier is important, as it can save you a significant amount of money. In the U.S., the largest decision you'll need to make is between UPS/FedEx and the U.S. Postal Service.

UPS/FEDEX – These privately run giants are great for shipping large, heavy packages domestically. Their rates for big shipments will be significantly lower than those charged by the USPS.

U.S. POSTAL SERVICE – If you're shipping small, lightweight items you can't beat the rates offered by the USPS. After dropshipping fees, the cheapest UPS shipping fee you're likely to see is around $10, while you can often ship items for $5 or less through the post office. The post office tends to be a better choice for sending international shipments, especially smaller ones. When setting up your shipping options, consider categorizing them by shipping

time ("Within 5 Days" or "Within 3 Days"), as this gives you the flexibility to pick the carrier that's the most economical for each order and delivery time.

Providing Customer Support

Take it from us: Managing all your customer emails, requests and returns in an Excel spreadsheet is NOT ideal. As excellent as Excel is, it's not built to handle customer support. Similarly, as your business and team grow, managing support with a single email inbox also quickly breaks down and leads to problems and service lapses. Implementing a help desk is one of the best things you can do to ensure quality

service for your customers. Help desk software comes in a number of different forms, but all provide a centralized location to manage your customer support correspondence and issues. Most desks make it easy to assign issues to team members and maintain communication history among all related parties.

A few popular options to choose from include:

HELP SCOUT – Less cluttered than other desks, Help Scout treats each issue as an email and removes all the traditionally appended ticket information that customers see with support requests. Instead, support tickets appear like standard emails to customers, creating a more personalized experience.

ZENDESK – Highly customizable and powerful, Zendesk offers a variety of tools and integrations and is one of the most popular help desks available. It takes some customization but is very powerful once it's tailored to your company.

DESK – Backed by well-known Sales Force, Desk's 'Universal Inbox' allows you to interact with your customers across numerous channels from one streamlined interface.

KAYAKO – Kayako boasts an all-in-one platform that offers built-in live chat, phone call and remote support issue management alongside traditional ticket based support.

Offering Phone Support

Deciding whether to offer phone support can be a tricky decision. It's obviously a great way to provide real-time support but is one of the most expensive support methods. If you're bootstrapping a business while working your 9 to 5, you won't be able to handle calls. But if you're working full-time on your business or have a staff member who can it might be a feasible option. If you're unable to staff a phone throughout the day, you can always have your phone number ring through to voicemail and return customer calls later. This isn't a perfect solution but can be a good compromise. You should consider the type of products you'll be selling when thinking about how to offer phone support. If you're a diamond boutique selling jewelry in the $1,000 to $5,000 range, many customers won't be comfortable placing an order that large without talking to a real person.

However, if you're selling products in the $25 to $50 range, most people will feel comfortable buying without phone support, assuming you've built a professional, information-rich website. If you do decide to offer phone support, think through strategic ways to do so 30.

Slapping a large 800 number on the top of every page can lead to a surfeit of low-value phone calls that cost more to support than they're worth. Instead, consider adding your number in more strategic places like the Contact Us and Shopping Cart pages, where you know the visitor has a high probability of purchasing.

Regardless of how you decide to handle sales requests, you should always be willing to call customers after the sale to resolve any issues that arise. There's nothing wrong with carefully evaluating the best ways to offer pre-sale support, but when it comes to taking care of people who have purchased from you, you should never refuse to help them on the phone.

The following services can help you set up a toll-free number and sales line:

Grasshopper31 – Grasshopper offers phone services and is geared toward smaller businesses and entrepreneurs. You can get a toll-free number, unlimited extensions, call forwarding and voicemail for a reasonable monthly fee (around $25).

RingCentral32 – RingCentral is the 800-pound gorilla in the VoIP and 800-number space, and we've used it in the past with mixed results. Its flexible interface lets you set up custom routing rules and extensions. For Mac users, I recommend looking for a different company unless you plan on buying a VoIP phone, as RingCentral's phone software for OS X is buggy and unreliable.

3. Specialize!

Almost every successful dropshipping store we encounter has one thing in common: It specializes in a certain product or niche. The more that stores specialize, the more successful they tend to be.

You don't want to just sell backpacks. You want to sell backpacks designed for around-the-world travelers obsessed with lightweight gear. You don't want to just sell security camera equipment. You want to focus on security systems for gas stations.

Many think narrowing their focus limits their potential customer base and will cost them sales. Just the opposite is true! Specializing allows you to communicate more effectively with your customers, stand out more easily from the competition and compete against a smaller field. Specializing is rarely a bad move to make in a dropshipping venture.

If you're launching a store in a new niche you probably won't know what segment of your customers to focus on – and that's OK. But as you gain experience with your customers you should identify the segment that's the most profitable and that allows you to add the most value. Then, try to position your business to focus exclusively on those customers' needs and problems. You'll be amazed at how your conversion rates skyrocket even if you're charging a premium price.

Remember: IF EVERYONE IS YOUR CUSTOMER, THEN NO ONE IS.

Specialization makes it easier to differentiate yourself, charge a premium price and concentrate your marketing efforts more effectively.

4. Have a Long-Term Perspective

Building a dropshipping business is like building anything else of value: It takes a significant level of commitment and investment over time. Yet for some reason people assume they can build a passive six-figure income with dropshipping after a few months of part-time work. That's just not the way it works.

As we mentioned in Starting Your Business, it will realistically take at least a year to build a business that generates an average full-time income. It's also important to understand that the first few months are the most difficult.

You'll struggle with doubts, run into issues with your website and will likely have an underwhelming website launch that generates zero sales. Understand that this is normal! Rome wasn't built in a day, and neither were any successful dropshipping businesses.

If you mentally prepare for a challenging beginning and don't expect to get rich overnight, you'll be much more likely to stick with your business until it becomes a success.

5. Offer Outstanding Service

The Internet has always been a fairly transparent place, but the recent rise of social media has made your business reputation even more important to your success online. If you don't treat your customers well, they'll often let the entire world know – including many potential customers.

The biggest customer service risk for dropshipping merchants is having tunnel vision on per-order profits and losses when fulfillment issues go awry. it's critical to accept that dropshipping can get messy, that you'll be paying to clean up some messes, and that you shouldn't always try to pass these on to your customer. If you aren't occasionally losing money on individual orders to make customers happy, you're probably not providing very good service.

Having happy customers is some of – if not THE – best marketing you can do. As is true in all businesses, it's much easier to make a sale to a satisfied customer than to try to convince a new prospect to buy. If you treat your profitability

customers exceptionally well, they're likely to spread the word and refer others your way. With top-notch service, you can build a business where repeat customers generate much of your revenue.

Making customer service a priority set your dropshipping business up for success, so ensure it's a priority from the outset.

6. Don't Get Hung Up on the Details

Don't focus too much on the details. Your company name, logo, theme or email marketing service aren't going to determine your success. What makes a business successful are the things we just talked about: adding value, marketing, outstanding customer service, specializing and a long-term commitment. Still, new merchants will spend weeks sometimes months struggling to make a decision between two shopping carts or providers. That's valuable time better spent developing the core aspects of the business.

Do your research and make an informed decision, but don't let small decisions Paralyze you.

7. The Most Important Step

The most important step the one that most people never take is to actually get started building your business! This is the hardest thing for most people and it's usually a result of fear and uncertainty.

It's a common misconception that successful entrepreneurs have a rock-solid certainty about their business at the outset. When you dig a little deeper, you'll find that most had fears and reservations about how things would turn out. Yet they moved forward with their plan despite these doubts.

If you're serious about building your own dropshipping business, you'll need to do the same. Do your research, evaluate your options and then move forward with that information in spite of your fears and reservations. It's what entrepreneurs do.

Tools & Add Ons To Create a Successful Dropshipping Business

Creating your Shopify website is the first step of creating a dropshipping website. In this section I will go over a few other tools and resource you may want to consider to forming your business. As previously mentioned these are recommendations and are optional but I highly recommend you form a legitimate business to protect your personal assets.

Register Your Dropshipping Business

After your dropshipping website is live I would recommend you create your business and form a Limited Liability Company (LLC), a Sole Proprietorship, or a C Corporation. I am not a lawyer so you will have to decide which business structure is best for you. If you plan on forming a business I would recommend to use My Company Works, these guys are experts and you can file all of the paperwork online. Again this is optional and most dropshippers do not file for a business.

I will not steer you in choosing a business structure but most small entrepreneurs usually file either a sole proprietorship or an LLC. Personally, I believe an LLC would be best for your dropshipping businesses because it offers liability protection, autonomy from personal finances and costs.

Request An EIN Number

You will also want to request an EIN number. The IRS requires all businesses to have an "Employer Identification Number". This acts as a social security number for your business. You'll need this number to file your taxes, and to open a bank account. This is a free and easy process and you can apply online.

Sign Up For A Business Credit Card

If you do decide to form a legal business, you should also apply for a business credit card, another Paypal account, and a business checking account. You will be making a lot of purchases to fulfill your dropship orders, so using a business credit card will help you keep personal and business expenses separate. You will also want a business credit card in case your supplier leaves the purchase order in the package, you would want the business name to be the buyer rather than your real name. You will want to have a PayPal account and a business checking account to keep track of your money made by the business. This way when you file your taxes, you will know exactly how much money your business made. Having a business credit card has great perks such as reward points and you can write purchases off on your taxes. I'm not an accountant but I encourage you to look into a term called "business expense", this can save you thousands of dollars come tax season, just make sure you keep your receipts.

To save you the hassle you do not have to do this, you can use your personal PayPal account and your personal credit card as many dropshippers do.

Collect Sales Tax

You will need to collect sales tax if both of the following statements are true:

· The state your business is located in collects sales tax and

· Someone living in your states places an order

Rather than adding sales tax to the end of the order, I would factor that price into the product for anyone who orders. Just make sure you are recording the orders purchased in the same state that you operate in, so you can pay the appropriate state tax. If someone places an order in a different state even if their state charges their own sales tax you won't need to charge them any tax. This is as of now, these tax laws are subject to change. To find out how to register as a retailer contact your state's Department of Commerce, and make sure to ask how often you need to submit the tax you collect and ask any other questions you may have regarding state tax.

CHAPTER THREE

DROPSHIPPING PRODUCTS AND SUPPLIERS

Where To Buy Your Dropshipping Products

If you're starting a dropshipping business or you already have a business like this, AliExpress is a great website to get the best deals. AliExpress offers thousands of products, free shipping, and low prices. Many of the top dropshippers use AliExpress to fulfill their orders just make sure you buy from trusted sellers to avoid any possible scams or mix-ups. Again this website is completely optional but I highly recommend going through them for all your orders.

Use Ali Express to buy your products and sell on Shopify.

Get A Phone Number For Your Dropshipping Business

If you are okay with giving out your personal number for your business then you can disregard this part. However, you can use your same cell phone and have a second number and also be able to send text messages from it. By using the app Burner App, you can have a real number for your business. For just

$4.99 a month, you can receive and make calls and send text messages, should a customer just has a quick question.

Get An Address For Your Dropshipping Business

Rent a PO Box online or at your local UPS store. That's right; you can rent a PO Box with a real address and use it for your business. I recommend using ipostal1.com because you can do everything online and have your own business address in just a few hours. This is a great option, to avoid people from knowing your personal address. Rather than renting a costly office space, you can rent a PO Box for as little as $9.99 a month.

If you are looking to save money and have the cheapest dropshipping business you can use your home address. If you are renting or live in an apartment you may want to double check with your landlord just in case.

Join Fiverr

Join the website Fiverr for any work you need done on your website. You can have someone on Fiverr write your content, build backlinks, or even design a logo. Most of the services cost as low as $5 and you can expect to get your work done in about a week or less. Make sure you read the reviews before using someone on Fiverr, you'll want someone with experience and great reviews. Most of the people on Fiverr speak another language so you should proofread all of the content before adding it to your website, granted you used the service for that.

Again you can write your own content and chances are it will be better and free, however, if you outsource it to Fiverr it will just save you time. So you need to consider what is more valuable to you, your time or saving money.

How to Spot Fake

Dropshipping Wholesalers

Depending on where you're searching, you'll likely come across a large number of "fake" wholesalers. Unfortunately legitimate wholesalers are traditionally poor at marketing and tend to be harder to find. This results in the non-genuine wholesalers – usually just middle men – appearing more frequently in your searches, so you'll want to be cautious.

The following tactics will help you discern whether a wholesale supplier is legitimate:

THEY WANT ONGOING FEES – Real wholesalers don't charge their customers a monthly fee for the privilege of doing business and ordering from them. If a supplier asks for a monthly membership

or service fee, it's likely not legitimate. It's important to differentiate here between suppliers and supplier directories. Supplier directories (which we'll discuss shortly) are directories of wholesale suppliers organized by product types or market and screened to ensure the suppliers are legitimate. Most directories will charge a fee – either one time or ongoing – so you shouldn't take this as a sign the directory itself is illegitimate.

Finding and Working With Suppliers

THEY SELL TO THE PUBLIC – To get genuine wholesale pricing you'll need to apply for a wholesale account, prove you're a legitimate business and be approved before placing your first order. Any wholesale supplier that offers products to the general public at "wholesale prices" is just a retailer offering items at inflated prices.

But here are some legitimate dropshipping fees you'll likely encounter:

PER-ORDER FEES – Many dropshippers will charge a per-order drop hipping fee that can range from $2 to $5 or more, depending on the size and complexity of the items being shipped. This is standard in the industry, as the costs of packing and shipping individual orders are much higher than shipping a bulk order.

MINIMUM ORDER SIZES – Some wholesalers will have a minimum initial order size, which is the lowest amount you have to purchase for your first order. They do this in order to filter out windowshopping merchants that will waste their time with questions and small orders but won't translate into meaningful business. If you're dropshipping, this could cause some complications. For example, what do you do if a supplier has a $500 minimum order, but your average order size is around $100? You don't want to pre-order $500 of product just for the privilege of opening a dropshipping account. In this situation, it's best to offer to pre-pay the supplier $500 to build a credit with them to apply against your drop shipping orders. This allows you to meet the supplier's minimum purchase requirement (as you're committing to buy at least $500 in product) without having to place a single large order without any corresponding customer orders.

Finding Wholesale Suppliers

Now that you can spot a fraud from the real deal, it's time to start searching for suppliers! You can use a number of different strategies, some more effective than others. The methods below are listed in order of effectiveness and preference, with my favorite methods listed first:

Contact the Manufacturer

This is my favorite way to easily locate legitimate wholesale suppliers. If you know the product(s) you want to sell, call the manufacturer and ask for a list of its wholesale distributors. You can then contact these wholesalers to see if they dropship and inquire about setting up an account. Since most wholesalers carry products from a variety of manufacturers, this strategy will allow you to quickly source a selection of products within the niche you're exploring. After making a couple of calls to the leading manufacturers in a niche, you'll quickly be able to identify the leading wholesalers in that market.

Search Using Google

Using Google to find high-quality suppliers may seem obvious, but there are a few rules to keep in mind:

1. YOU HAVE TO SEARCH EXTENSIVELY – Wholesalers are terrible at marketing and promotion, and they're definitely not going to top the search results for "wholesale suppliers for product X." This means you'll

likely have to dig through LOTS of search results —
possibly hundreds — to find the wholesaler's website
listed way down at #55.

2. DON'T JUDGE BY THE WEBSITE — Wholesalers are
also notorious for having poorly designed '90s-style
websites. So while a quality site may indicate a good
supplier in some cases, many legitimate wholesalers
have cringe-worthy homepages. Don't let the poor
design scare you off.

3. USE LOTS OF MODIFIERS — Wholesalers aren't
doing extensive SEO to ensure you find their websites,
so you might need to try various search queries. Don't
stop at just "[product] wholesaler." Try using
modifiers such as "distributor," "reseller," "bulk,"
"warehouse" and "supplier."

Order From the Competition

If you're having a hard time locating a supplier, you
can always use the old order-from-the-competition
trick. Here's how it works: Find a competitor you
think is dropshipping and place a small order with
that company. When you receive the package, Google
the return address to find out who the original
shipper was. In some cases, it will be a supplier you
can contact. This is a tactic I've heard discussed by
others but haven't used myselves. And if you haven't

been able to find a supplier using the other techniques discussed above, there might be a good reason (i.e., the market is too small, there's not enough demand to justify a supplier, etc.). So keep this technique in mind, but don't rely too heavily on it.

Attend a Trade Show

A trade show allows you to connect with all the major manufacturers and wholesalers in a niche. It's a great way to make contacts and research your products and suppliers all in one spot. This only works if you've already selected your niche and/or product, and it isn't feasible for everyone. But if you have the time and money to attend, it's a great way to get to know the manufactures and suppliers in a market.

Directories

One of the most common questions aspiring ecommerce entrepreneurs ask is:

Should I pay for a supplier directory?

A supplier directory is a database of suppliers that's organized by market, niche or product. Many directories employ some sort of screening process to ensure the suppliers listed are genuine wholesalers. Most are run by for-profit companies who charge a fee for access to their directory.

While membership directories can be helpful, especially for brainstorming ideas, they are by no means necessary. If you already know the product or niche you want to sell, you should be able to find the major suppliers in your market with a bit of digging and the techniques discussed above. Plus, once you start your business you likely won't need to revisit the directory unless you need to find suppliers for other products. That said, supplier directories are a convenient way to quickly search for and/or browse a large number of suppliers in one place and are great for brainstorming ideas for products to sell or niches to enter. If you're short on time and are willing to spend the money, they can be a helpful tool.

There are a number of different supplier directories, and a comprehensive review of all of them is beyond the scope of this guide. Instead, I've highlighted some of the most well-known supplier directories online. Please note I'm not endorsing any of these directories, i'm simply providing you

with some options.

Worldwide Brands

www.worldwidebrands.com

Quick Stats:

• Established 1999

• Thousands of wholesalers

• Over 10 million products

• Price: $299 for a lifetime membership

Worldwide Brands is one of the oldest and best-known supplier directories. It advertises that it only includes suppliers that meet a set of guidelines to ensure legitimate, quality wholesalers. I've used the directory in the past to find legitimate wholesalers and to brainstorm niche ideas – and found it useful. Though the directory is missing some suppliers I've worked with, it does include a large collection of legitimate wholesalers. If you want lifetime access to a quality directory and are comfortable with a larger one-time payment, Worldwide Brands is a safe bet.

SaleHoo

www.salehoo.com

Quick Stats:

• Established 2005

• Over 8,000 suppliers

• Price: $67 per year

The SaleHoo supplier directory lists more than 8,000 bulk-purchase and dropshipping suppliers, and seems to cater heavily to merchants on eBay, and Amazon.

Although I've never used SaleHoo to source products, its $67 annual

price is one of the most compelling values among supplier directories and includes a 60-day money-back guarantee. If you're comfortable paying an annual membership – or only need to use a directory temporarily -SaleHoo might be worth a look.

Doba

www.doba.com

Quick Stats:

• Established 2002

• 165 suppliers

• Over 1.5 million products

• Price: $60 per month

Instead of simply listing suppliers, Doba's service integrates withdropshippers (hence why they only have 165 suppliers) allowing you to place orders with multiple warehouses using its centralized interface.

Membership also includes a Push-to-Marketplace tool that automates the process of listing items on eBay.

Doba's centralized system offers more convenience then the other directories which is why I imagine the $60 / month fee is significantly higher than other prices. If you place a high value on convenience and can find the products you want among their suppliers, Doba's interface may be worth the cost.

However, if you can identify quality suppliers on your own and don't mind working with them directly, you'll be able to save around $700 / year. If there are only a few key suppliers in your niche – reducing the number of parties you have to coordinate with – this may be the way to go.

Wholesale Central

www.wholesalecentral.com

Quick Stats:

• Established 1996

• 1,400 suppliers

• 740,000 products

• Price: free

Unlike many other directories, there's no charge to search Wholesale Central for suppliers because it charges suppliers a fee to be listed and also displays ads on their site. They also claim to review and screen all suppliers to ensure they are legitimate and trustworthy. It's difficult to argue with free, and there's no harm in browsing the listings at Wholesale Central, but you'll need to be a bit more discriminating. A number of the suppliers I found appeared to be retailers selling to the public at "wholesale" prices – not something a supplier would do when offering real wholesale pricing. So while I'm sure there are genuine wholesale opportunities listed, you may want to be a little more thorough with your due diligence. Alright, so you've found a number of solid suppliers and are ready to move forward – great! But before you start contacting companies, you'll want to have all your ducks in a row.

There are many websites to find cheap wholesalers and suppliers, when just starting out the easiest to use in my opinion is Ali Express. There are many sellers on the website as well as many products to choose from so it can be overwhelming. I would recommend a product that has fewer than 100,000 monthly searches on Google; you can use the keyword planner or install the Google Chrome extension called "keywords everywhere" to easily get the search volume for products. If you are still unsure about the product you want to sell that's okay, I will have a handful of suggestions you can use, but ultimately the decision on what you sell is yours.

You can also use Ali express

If you choose to use Ali Express for your dropshipping business, there are many filters you may use to find reliable suppliers. You can add filters for seller reviews (4 stars and up), free shipping, lowest price, and domestic returns. You can even get other information about the company such as how many years they were in business, the total orders and dollar amount they have sold, which type of payment they accept, and their shipping windows/options. The most important to me would be the seller's rating, you want someone you can trust and who will fulfill your orders. Make sure they have more than one good review, because let's be honest it's very easy to have someone write a fake review for you.

Stay In Constant Contact With Your Supplier(s)

Don't be afraid to email and or call the supplier. If you plan on being a dropshipper for a long time, you need to build a relationship with your supplier. This is a win-win situation for both parties if it works correct, meaning both of you will potentially be making money. If you don't get a response in a reasonable amount of time usually 24–72 hours, you might want to send a follow-up email or call. Keep in mind most of the sellers on Ali Express are overseas so they may not have as much access to the internet as you and I. Reach out to more than one supplier, best case they all answer back and then you can test the quality of the product(s) out. I highly recommend you pay or request a free sample so you can evaluate the packaging of the product, the delivery time, and the quality of the product. You won't have much of a dropshipping business if your supplier does not meet your expectations.

How to Appear as a dropshipper

YOU NEED TO BE LEGAL – As I mentioned earlier, most legitimate wholesalers will require proof that you're a legal business before allowing you to apply for an account. Most wholesalers only reveal their pricing to approved customers, so you'll need to be legally incorporated before you'll get to see the kind of pricing you'll receive. Bottom line? Make sure you're legally incorporated before contacting suppliers!

If you're only looking to ask a few basic questions ("Do you drop ship?" "Do you carry brand X?"), you won't need to provide any documentation. But don't expect to launch without having your business properly set up.

UNDERSTAND HOW YOU APPEAR – Wholesalers are constantly bombarded by people with "great business plans" who pepper them with questions, take up a lot time and then never order anything. So if you're launching a new business, be aware that many suppliers aren't going to go out of their way to help you get started.

Most will be happy to set you up with a dropshipping account if they offer it. But don't ask for discount pricing or spend hours tying up their sales representatives on the phone before you've made a single sale. It will quickly earn you a bad reputation and hurt your relationship with the supplier. If you do need to make special requests (say, trying to convince a supplier to dropship when it normally doesn't), you need to build credibility. Be definitive about your business plans ("We ARE launching this site on January 20) instead of using flaky rhetoric ("I'm thinking about maybe launching a business sometime soon"). And be sure to communicate any professional successes you've had in the past – especially with sales and marketing – that will help you with your new venture.

You need to convince suppliers that the inconvenience of accommodating your special request(s) will pay off down the road when you become successful and start bringing them a ton of business.

DON'T BE AFRAID OF THE PHONE – One of the biggest fears people have when it comes to suppliers is simply picking up the phone and making the call. For many, this is a paralyzing prospect. You might be able to send emails for some issues, but more often than not you'll need to pick up the phone to get the information you need.

The good news is that it's not as scary as you might think. Suppliers are accustomed to having people call them, including newbie entrepreneurs. You're likely to get someone who's friendly and more than happy to answer your questions. Here's a tip that will help you, simply write out your questions ahead of time. It's amazing how much easier it is to make the call when you've got a list of pre-written questions to ask.

Qualities of a Good Suppliers

Like most things in life, suppliers are not all created equally. In the world of dropshipping – where the supplier is such a critical part of your fulfillment process – it's even more important to make sure you're working with top-notch players. Great suppliers tend to have many of the following 6 attributes:

EXPERT STAFF AND INDUSTRY FOCUS – Top-notch suppliers have knowledgeable sales representatives who really know the industry and their product lines. Being able to call a representative with questions is invaluable, especially if you're launching a store in a niche you're not overly familiar with.

DEDICATED SUPPORT REPRESENTATIVES – Quality dropshippers should assign you an individual sales representative responsible for taking care of you and any issues you have. We've dealt with wholesalers that don't assign specific representatives and we hate it. Problems take a lot longer to resolve, and we usually have to nag people to take care of an issue. Having a single supplier contact who's responsible for solving your issues is really important.

INVESTED IN TECHNOLOGY – While there are plenty of good suppliers with outdated websites, a supplier that understands the benefits of – and invests heavily in – technology is usually a pleasure to work with. Features such as real-time inventory, a comprehensive online catalog, customizable data feeds and an online searchable order history are pure luxury for online merchants and can help you streamline your operations.

CAN TAKE ORDERS VIA EMAIL – This may sound like a minor issue, but having to call every order in – or manually place it on the website – makes processing orders significantly more time intensive.

CENTRALLY LOCATED – If you're in a large country like the United States, it's beneficial to use a centrally located dropshipper, as packages can reach more than 90% of the country within 2 to 3 business days. When a supplier is located on one of the coasts, it can take more than a week for orders to be shipped across the country. Centrally located suppliers allow you to consistently promise faster delivery times, potentially saving you money on shipping fees.

ORGANIZED AND EFFICIENT – Some suppliers have competent staff and great systems that result in efficient and mostly error-free fulfillment. Others will botch every fourth order and make you want to tear your hair out. The trouble is, it's difficult to know how competent a supplier is without actually using it. Although it won't give you a complete picture, placing a few small test orders can give you a great sense of how a supplier operates. You can see:

• How they handle the order process

• How quickly the items ship out

• How rapidly they follow up with tracking information and an invoice

• The quality of the pack job when the item arrives

Your Options on Paying Suppliers

The vast majority of suppliers will accept payment in one of two ways:

Credit Card

When you're starting out, most suppliers will require you to pay by credit card. Once you've established a thriving business, paying with credit cards is often still the best option. They're not only convenient (no need to write checks regularly), but you can rack up a LOT of rewards points/frequent flier miles. Because you're buying a product for a customer who has already paid for it on your website, you can rack up a high volume of purchases through your credit card without having to incur any actual out-of-pocket expenses.

Net Terms

The other common way to pay suppliers is with "net terms" on invoice. This simply means that you have a certain number of days to pay the supplier for the goods you've purchased. So if you're on "net 30" terms, you have 30 days from the date of purchase to pay your supplier – by check or bank draw – for the goods you bought. Usually, a supplier will make you provide credit references before offering net payment terms because it's effectively lending you money. This is a common practice, so don't be alarmed if you have to provide some documentation when paying on net terms.

The biggest hurdle most new dropshipping entrepreneurs face is picking a niche and products to focus on. And it's understandable – it's likely the biggest decision you'll make and has long-term consequences on the success or failure of the business.

The most common mistake at this stage is picking a product based on personal interest or passion. This is an acceptable strategy if being interested in the product is your primary objective, not necessarily business success. But if your #1 goal is to build a profitable dropshipping site, you'll want to consider setting your personal passions aside 1 when doing market research, or at least making sure they meet with the criteria discussed below.

Picking The Best Dropshipping Products

Finding the right product to sell can be hard; fortunately we are here to help you find the best products to dropship in 2018 and beyond. This next section is going to cover a lot of information including how to find the right product to sell, how to write quality content on your website, and how to get traffic to your website. If you have stayed with me this far, I will share some ideas on products you can dropship and I will also share some free websites that you can get high authority backlinks from (one of the most important factors for ranking on Google).

Picking the right product to dropship.

Niche Products Tend To Be The Best To Dropship

Picking the right product can be challenging, this is ultimately what makes your dropshipping business. If you pick a product that you are passionate about, but no one else is than you are likely not going to be around long. If you pick a popular product with a lot of monthly searches you probably will never rank high on Google, lead to people not finding your website. You need to find a niche or in simpler terms a very specific product that's has a very specific audience. In this section I will show you how to find products to sell online by using free tools on Google. I think it's important to start a business you are passionate about, because then it won't feel like a job and will be very easy and natural to write high quality content. But dropshipping is a different beast, you need to find a niche maybe boring product that you can buy from a supplier at a low cost and then sell in the US for a higher price. When it comes to dropshipping you need to be passionate about making money and you can even have someone write your content for as cheap as $5 on Fiverr. I personally write all my own content, because I'm cheap and practical but for $5 it might be worth it to have someone on Fiverr write for you, especially if it's a dull topic. Just a warning be prepared to proofread any work that you outsource, some of these people are from overseas where English is not their first language.

Other Considerations When Selecting Products

THE PERFECT PRICE – Make sure you strongly consider the price point relative to the level of pre-sale service you'll need to provide. Most people feel comfortable placing a $200 order online without talking to someone on the phone. But what about a $1,500 item they're unfamiliar with? Chances are, most would want to chat directly with a sales representative before making such a large purchase, both to ensure the item is a good fit and to make sure the store is legitimate. If you plan to sell high-priced items, make sure you're able to offer personalized phone support. You'll also want to ensure that the margins are rich enough to justify the pre-sale support you'll need to offer. Often, the $50 to $200 price range is the sweet spot to maximize revenue without having to provide extensive pre-sale support.

MAP PRICING – Some manufacturers will set what's

called a minimum advertised price (MAP) for their products, and require that all resellers price their products at or above certain levels. This pricing floor prevents the price wars that often break out – especially for products that are easily drop shipped – and helps ensure that merchants can make a reasonable profit by carrying a manufacturer's products.

CHAPTER FOUR

HOW TO BUILD STORE AND GET RIGHT CUSTOMERS

How To Build A Successful Shopify Store

Selling at the lowest prices: Selling your products at a lower cost than the competition is a very common strategy. Unfortunately, this won't always work with every product. Price is very important, so I encourage you to keep your prices reasonable but you need to offer more than low prices to build trust with someone. Getting a pricing war will not go over too well, especially for a small dropshipping business. Amazon and Walmart can easily talk to their wholesalers to get a lower price if you steal too much of their business away and heck they might even lower their price and sell the product at a loss just to get people to their website or physical stores. Yes, billion dollar companies can destroy you easily.

Add Value: I cannot stress this enough, adding value should be just as important to you as getting a sale. Once you start selling online, you'll be amazed that some people will buy from you even if your prices are higher. Because you provided them something the rest of the competition didn't. One of the easiest ways to add value is by writing long content that describes the product and all the benefits your product can offer that customer. I recommend you even make a short video on YouTube for each product you sell, people love engaging in content, before making a purchase.

People tend to go to Google or other search engines when they have a question or a problem they need to solve. So building your content to solve their question or need is going to lead to sales. To further explain, let's say I'm looking for a cool keychain your content should explain what a cool keychain is, its benefits, the price, and the options I can chose from (design, why it's cool, color, size, logo, etc). You want to make the customer's decision and choice as easy as possible. Sometimes adding value is as easy as selling every possible color keychain available, and by doing this price may not be as important.

Customer Service: Having great customer service is a great skill to have. It's very refreshing to be able to call someone or email a business if and when I should have a question or concern about a product. If you are a small dropshipping company with one or two employees it will be hard to have 24 hour customer service, but being responsive and answering every inquiry will help your business excel. Excellent customer service will help you sell more even if you have a higher price than the competition. Being there for your customers really matters.

Quality Images & Videos: You'll want to have high quality product images on your site, that truly represent what the product looks like, trust me no one likes being lied to. As a consumer it's very annoying when a seller uses stock images and then you get a product and it looks nothing like the product in the image. I recommend you buy the product and take your own pictures with a good camera. When and if you record a video demonstrating the product, make sure you have crystal clear video and that it's easy to hear. You'll want to differentiate yourself from the competition so make sure the pictures of your dropshipping products stand out!

Educate your customers: Let's say you are dropshipping a product such as a "door draft stopper". Some people may not know what that is, but it's a piece of plastic and fiber that you attach under your door to prevent a draft your house. Talk about a great niche product to dropship "wink wink". Now this is a great way for you to purchase the product and record yourself putting together and installing under your door. This will help educate your customer, build your reputation, and create value. If videos aren't your thing, you can take picture of each step on how to install a door draft stopper and then write a short paragraph under each image to really help your end user.

Upsell Products: Upselling products is one of the easiest ways to make more money. Let's say you are selling "microfiber car towels" . These are extremely soft towels used to dry after you wash your car, here is your chance to sell car wax or another product to help with the car washing process. This is how you build a name for yourself and eventually you can scale your business to becoming the one stop shop for all your car wash needs. But everything takes time, so give yourself a chance; success doesn't happen overnight.

Dropshipping products

Here a few niche products that you can start your dropshipping business with. If you noticed a few were mentioned above. These all sell for pretty cheap on Ali Express and most offer great margins of over 100% and even leave room to upsell other products down the line. All of these products have fewer than 50,000 monthly searches on Google, which make them perfect to try to rank for on search engines. Ranking on Google and getting traffic to your website is not guaranteed so that part is solely on you and your marketing efforts; these are just some dropshipping ideas to help you get started. Again this is just my opinion on the best items to dropship.

· Cool keychains

· Door draft stopper

· Microfiber car towels

· Dust pans with/without brooms

· Snoring chin straps

· Eye mask

Selling a product

with many accessories is a great way to improve your overall margin. If you can find a niche where manufacturers enforce MAP pricing it's a huge benefit, especially if you plan on building a high-value and information-rich site. With prices the same across all competitors, you can compete on the strength of your website and won't have to worry about losing business to less reputable but cheaper competition.

MARKETING POTENTIAL – The time to think about how you'll market a business is before you launch it, not three months in when you realize that customer acquisition is a nightmare. Can you brainstorm a number of ways you could promote your store by, for example, writing articles, giving away products or reaching out to active online communities that use the products you're selling? If not, you may want to reconsider.

LOTS OF ACCESSORIES – As a general rule of retail, margins on lower priced accessories are significantly higher than those of highpriced items. While a cell phone store may only make a 5% margin on the latest smartphone, they'll almost certainly make a 100% or 200% margin on the case that goes with it.

As customers, we're also much more sensitive about the price on a big-ticket item and care less about the price of smaller accessories. To use the previous example, you'd likely shop around for the best price on an expensive smartphone. But are you going to call around to find the best price on a $20 to $30 case? Probably not. You'll likely purchase it from the same store where you bought the phone.

LOW TURNOVER – I hope you're convinced by now that investing in an education-rich, high-quality site will pay big dividends. But if the products you sell change every year, maintaining that site is quickly going to turn into a mountain of work. Try to find products that aren't updated with new models every year. That way, the time and money you invest in a superb site will last longer.

HARD TO FIND LOCALLY – Selling a product that's hard to find locally will increase your chances of success as long as you don't get too specific. Most people needing a garden rake or a sprinkler would simply run down to the local hardware store. But where would you buy a medieval knight's costume or falcon training equipment? You'd probably head to Google and start searching.

SMALLER IS USUALLY BETTER – In a world where free shipping is often expected, it can be a challenge to sell large, heavy equipment that's expensive to ship. The smaller the items, the easier they are to ship cheaply to your customers.

Picking a profitable niche isn't easy and requires you to consider numerous factors. These guidelines should give you a good idea of the types of drop shipped products that work well. Without demand, it doesn't matter if your niche fits 100% of the attributes listed above. If nobody wants your product, you'll have a hard time making any money! As the old saying goes, it's much easier to fill existing demand than to try to create it.

Fortunately, a number of online tools allow you to

measure demand for a product or market. The most well-known and popular is the Google Keyword Tool.

Measuring Demand

Google Keyword Tool

The best way to measure demand for an item online is to see how many people are searching for it using a search engine like Google. Fortunately, Google makes this search volume publicly available via its keyword tool. Simply type in a word or phrase, and the tool tells you how many people are searching for it every month.

Keep the following three tips in mind, and you'll be well on your way to getting the most out of the tool:

MATCH TYPE – The tool will let you select broad, phrase or exact match types when it reports search volumes. Unless you have a good reason to do otherwise, you should use the exact match option. This will give you a much more accurate picture of the applicable search volume for the keyword.

SEARCH LOCATION – Make sure you look at the difference between local

search volume (in your country or a user-defined region) and global search volumes. If you'll be selling primarily in the U.S., you should focus on the local search volumes and ignore the global results, as that's where most of your customers will be.

LONG-TAIL VARIATIONS – It's easy to fixate on the broad, one- or two-word search terms that get massive amounts of search volume. In reality, it's the longer, more specific and lower volume search queries that will make up most of your traffic from the search engines. These longer, more detailed search terms are commonly referred to as "long-tail" searches. Keep this in mind when you're looking at potential markets and niches to enter. If a search term has many variations that are actively searched for, that's a good sign that the market is fairly deep with lots of variety and interest. But if search queries and related volume drop off precipitously after the first few high-level words, there's probably less related long-tail traffic.

Google Trends

The keyword tool is great for raw search figures, but for more detailed insights you'll want to use Google Trends. The tool offers you information that the Keyword Tool just doesn't provide, including:

SEARCH VOLUME OVER TIME: Ideally, you want the niche you're entering to be growing and Trends can let you know if this is the case. For any given search query, you can see the growth or decline in search volume over time.

Below is a chart of search volume for the term "smartphone". As expected, search volume has risen sharply in the last few years:

TOP AND RISING TERMS: You'll also be able to get a snapshot at the most popular related searches, and which queries have been growing in popularity the fastest. Focusing on these popular and quickly growing terms can be helpful when planning your marketing and SEO efforts. According to the charts below, search queries related to AT&T, Verizon and Samsung seem to be experiencing the most growth in the smart phone market – data which shows up when we analyze the term "smartphone":

GEOGRAPHICAL CONCENTRATION: Another useful feature is the ability to see where people are searching for a term geographically. This can help you identify where your customer base for a niche is most heavily concentrated. For example, if you're selling canoes the charts below can help you determine that the majority of your customers will likely come from the Northern U.S., Alaska and Hawaii. If you were trying to decide between multiple suppliers, this knowledge could help you partner with one closest to the majority of your customers:

SEASONALITY: Understanding the seasonality of a market – that is, if the demand for a product changes dramatically at different points in the year – is crucially important. Because the keyword tool provides data on a monthly basis, you can draw some misleading conclusions if you measure search volumes during the wrong time of year. Revisiting our previous example, we can see below that "canoes" are a very seasons search term with demand peaking in the summer months. If you measured demand in the summer expecting that it would be constant throughout the year, you'd grossly overestimate the size of demand:

For any product you're seriously considering, you'll want to spend time understanding the intricacies of the niche's search volume. Using the Google Trend tool to understand search volumes, geographic concentration, high-level search trends and seasonality will offer insights that can help you avoid costly mistakes and optimize your marketing efforts. Conducting competitive analysis on a potential market can be tricky. Too much competition and you'll have difficulty building traffic and competing with established players. Too little competition can indicate a tiny market that will drastically limit how big you'll be able to grow.

Finding The Right Customer For Your Dropshipping Business

Finding the right customer can be hard at first, but in the digital marketing era we have now, there are many ways to get customers. There are paid options and free options available, if you chose paid make sure your product is priced correctly to factor in the extra expense. The best way is SEO, this is writing detailed content that fully explains and helps potentially customers find your website. This is writing content that has your keywords that are focused on sprinkled through your information. You do not want to over use that keyword because you will be penalized by Google for "keyword stuffing". Large orders are great, but if you are running an ecommerce site most people only will buy one maybe two products, so this market really will make the bulk of your business. Repeat orders are a beautiful thing so adding value and have great customer service will definitely make someone feel comfortable buying from you again.

Find the right customer for your product.

How To Get Traffic To Your Dropshipping Website

I want to share some light on how to get traffic to your website. If you want to learn more about anyone of these topics I recommend you check out moz.com, searchengineland.com, or use Google and search "SEO" or "how to run Facebook ads".

Learn how to get traffic to your website.

1. SEO/Blogging: Search engine optimization is optimizing your webpage or blog posts to rank on search engines. This means you write content about certain keywords you wish to rank for. Writing detailed and organized content that is. Then you want to create backlinks to your website. But if you just created a new website on Shopify, for this example you will want to create backlinks in moderation, you don't want to throw a ton of backlinks to your website and get a penalty by Google. Backlinks or referring domains simply means other websites that link back to yours. Generally higher quality backlinks will give your website more authority and more "SEO juice". Below are a few high authority website that you can get an easy backlink from. I encourage you to find an expert in SEO on Fiverr or to do some research on Google to learn more.

2. Posting on social media: Here is one of my favorite ways to get traffic to your website. Simply post your link on Facebook, in Facebook groups, Twitter, Instagram, LinkedIn, Pinterest, Snapchat, and any other social media accounts. This is a great way to

promote your website and it's free. Provide a small paragraph of what your website is about add your link and post it to your friends and followers. I also recommend you add the link to your bio on Instagram, Facebook, Twitter, and as a "job" on your LinkedIn account.

3. Creating YouTube videos: If you are serious about making this dropshipping business a success making a YouTube video every day is ideal. However, this can get tedious and you may run out of information but at least one video a week is a good start. When you post a YouTube video make sure you assign a title with the keyword or phrase you want to rank for and then write a nice description and add the link to your website. This is a great way to get traffic and views to your website and YouTube is the second largest search engine in the world, so being on there matters.

4. Facebook Ads: Facebook is the largest social media platform in the world. I recommend you create a Facebook business page for your website. Most successful dropshipping businesses run Facebook ads because they work, results may vary and these ads may not work for everybody. Once you create a "business page" you can set up and run paid ads on Facebook. The best part is you can cater your ads to a very specific audience. You can custom your audience

by age, interests, and other demographics. From from my experience the costs per click on Facebook can be as low as $.35 a click which is extremely cost effective.

5. Google Adwords: Running pay per click ads are a great way to get traffic to your website. Google lets you bid on keywords that you want to show up for. You enter a budget and the maximum amount of money you are willing to pay for a click. When someone clicks on your ad they will be sent to your website and you "pay per click". This is a bit more expensive than Facebook ads, but can be very profitable if done correctly. You can also cater your ads to serve to a specific market such as location, time of day, and keywords/phrases they are searching for online.

6. Other paid ads: There are other paid advertisements you can run on Bing, YouTube, Instagram, Pinterest, Twitter, and LinkedIn. I haven't had much experience with those ads so if you are interested in those channels I would look it up on Google and read few books regarding these topics.

7. Other Free Sources: I also recommend you post your content on Medium.com, this is the only website online to my knowledge that allows you to copy your content word for word without getting a penalty for

duplicate content. Medium is a great website to use because it has a high domain authority that you can leverage when creating a blog. At the end of each Medium post, add a link back to your website. Another great source to get traffic to your website is by answering questions on Quora.com. This is a site where users can ask and answer questions. Take the time to provide quality answers to other user's questions and link to your website when applicable.

Free Backlinks For Your Dropshipping Website

Here is a list of high authority backlinks that you can use, to improve your SEO rankings. Add a few sentences about your website and then add your link and there you go, you will get a backlink back to your website. For SEO ranking the more backlinks the better, but aim for quality websites not just quantity. I encourage you to read other websites to find out how to get high quality backlinks. Remember when you create your website on Shopify, your website will be brand new so add backlinks gradually so you don't risk getting a penalty. SEO is an ongoing battle so to rank higher on Google you will always need to find quality backlink opportunities and to write great content.

List Of Free Backlinks

· http://ttlink.com/

· https://medium.com/

· https://www.emoneyspace.com/

· http://www.apsense.com/start

· https://onmogul.com/

· https://steemit.com

Keyword Research Tools

To find the right keywords to try to rank for you can use a few different tools to get the monthly search volume of keywords or phrases. Every successful dropshipping business needs to focus on their niche keywords, so I recommend this website to find keyword ideas.

You can download the chrome extension called "Keywords Everywhere", once installed any keyword or phrase you enter on Google the extension will tell you the monthly search volume.

I would also recommend Google keyword planner and keyword.io to find the search volume of a larger list of keywords and you can also get recommendations of other related keywords.

Identify Other Dropshippers Or Competitor Websites

Doing keyword research is the first step, the next step would be to go to Google and type in the keyword you would like to rank for. The first 3–5 websites that show up organically are the websites you want to do your research on. You will want to see what products are on these pages, their price point and more important how long the content is. When writing content I really like the "skyscraper method", this is using the content from other websites but completely rewriting it so you aren't plagiarizing any content. You will also want to make your content longer than theirs to potentially rank higher. Simply copy all the words on that page and paste it into a word document to get the word count, then you will know how long you need to make your content.

How to Be Successful Selling Online

To build a successful ecommerce business, you'll need to do one of the

following:

MANUFACTURE YOUR OWN PRODUCT – You control distribution and are the sole source for the item. This limits competition and allows you to charge a premium price. If you intend to dropship products, you'll be selling existing products manufactured by someone else, so this isn't an option.

HAVE ACCESS TO EXCLUSIVE PRICING OR DISTRIBUTION – If you can arrange an exclusive agreement to carry a product – or if you have access to exclusive pricing from a manufacturer – you can profitably sell online without creating your own product. These arrangements can be difficult to arrange, Picking Products to Dropship

SELL AT THE LOWEST PRICE – If you can offer the lowest price, you'll likely steal business from a large chunk of the market. The only problem? It's a business model doomed to failure. If the only thing of value you have to offer is a low price, you'll be caught in a pricing war that will strip virtually all your profits. Trying to compete against Amazon and other established online giants on price is generally a poor strategy.

ADD VALUE IN NON-PRICING TERMS – Offering valuable information that complements your products is the BEST way to differentiate yourself and charge a premium price. Entrepreneurs set out to solve people's problems, and that's no different in the world of ecommerce and dropshipping. Offering expert advice and guidance within your niche is the best way to build a profitable dropshipping business.

ADDING VALUE IN ECOMMERCE – Just add value! Simple enough, right? Well, that's easier said than done. Some products and niches lend themselves to this strategy more than others. You should look for a few key characteristics that make adding value with educational content much easier. Specially, you'll want to look for niches that:

HAVE MANY COMPONENTS – The more components a product needs to function properly, the more likely customers are to turn to the internet for answers. Which purchase is more confusing: buying a new office chair or buying a home security camera system that requires multiple cameras, complex wiring and a recorder?

The more components a product needs – and the more variety among those components – the greater your opportunity to add value by advising customers on which products are compatible.

ARE CUSTOMIZABLE/CONFUSING – Along the same vein, confusing and customizable products are perfect for adding value through content. Would you inherently know how to select the best hot water solar panel configuration for your climate or which type of wireless dog collar system is right for your yard? Being able to offer specific guidance on what types of products are best suited for specific

JONATHAN BECKER

environments and customers is a great way to add value.

REQUIRE TECHNICAL SETUP OR INSTALLATION – It's easy to offer expert guidance for products that are difficult to set up, install or assemble. Take the security camera system from before. Let's say the camera site had a detailed 50-page installation guide that also covered the most common mistakes people make installing their own systems. If you thought the guide could save you time and hassle, there's a good chance you'd buy it from that website even if it was available for a few dollars less elsewhere. For store owners, the guides add tremendous value to customers and don't cost anything to provide once they're created.

Ways to Add Value:

You can add value to complex and confusing niches in a number of ways, including:

• Creating comprehensive buyers' guides

• Investing in detailed product descriptions and listings

• Creating installation and setup guides (as discussed above)

• Creating in-depth videos showing how the product works

• Establishing an easy-to-follow system for understanding component compatibility

Cherry-Picking the Best Customers

All customers aren't created equally. It's strange how some customers buying small items feel entitled to demand the moon while other big spenders rarely ask for anything. Targeting the right demographic can be a big boon for your business. These clients tend to make it worth your while:

HOBBYISTS – People love their hobbies and will spend mind-boggling amounts on equipment, training and tools for them. Many serious mountain bikers have bikes that cost more than their cars, and folks who love to fish might spend a fortune outfitting their boats. If you can target the right hobbyist niche and successfully connect with enthusiasts and their needs, you can do very well.

BUSINESSES – Business clients are sometimes more price-sensitive but will almost always order in larger quantities than individual consumers. Once you've established a rapport and earned their trust, you open the door to a long-term, high-volume profitable relationship. If at all possible, try to sell products that appeal to both individual customers and businesses.

REPEAT BUYERS – Recurring revenue is a beautiful thing. If you sell products that are disposable and/or need to be reordered frequently, you can grow rapidly as you build a loyal customer base that frequently returns to purchase.

Become a professional dropshipper

Do your homework on your competition, research your keywords/products, and find as much information online as possible on running your business. Once you think you are ready, make your best decision and go for it. If you put off starting your dropshipping business waiting for the perfect product and the perfect market you'll probably never get started.

More About Dropshipping

* Some so-called dropshipping offers border on scams, asking a high fee to access a site, where you'll find more firms offering dropshipping information who in turn ask payment to access their sites, and so on, and so on. Where products are accessible with graphics and sales materials for your eBay listings, oftentimes the goods are rubbish, sometimes they're

grossly overpriced. They might be seconds, end of line, customer returns, damaged... you get the picture!

* That said, there are many excellent paid-for membership sites offering sound contact details for worldwide dropshipping companies. Some membership sites continuously scrutinise their recommended suppliers, and score entries 1 to 5, acceptable to excellent, based on member feedback. The best we found, Worldwide Brands, is eBay acknowledged and operated by Chris Malta, Product Sourcing Editor of eBay Radio. The company has a team of researchers on constant lookout for new dropshipping and wholesale suppliers to add to their directory.

* Find dropshipping companies yourself via their own advertisements in local newspapers (not national; too competitive), at trade shows, by word of mouth from sellers of non-competing products. Search for them online via search engines such as http://www.google.com (our preference); use appropriate keywords like 'manufacturers dolls (or other product) New York (or other location)'.

* Look for firms selling lots of different products, on a related or unrelated theme. Within hours of deciding to sell dog featured jewelry, I searched

http://www.google.com and found two firms willing to dropship their wide ranging products to our customers, with no minimum order, and a CD of graphics and sales materials arriving next day. Another firm, based a few miles from us, has more than twelve different products for over 100 breeds of dog, and no one currently selling their products on eBay! No graphics either, so we checked their products, bought one of each, and created our own unique listings.

* Typically you pay the supplier an agreed amount per shipment upfront, although some will invoice you later. For local firms you can pop down, offer their share, hand over delivery labels. When you have a good supplier, ask permission to pack goods yourself at their premises so you can insert special offer flyers, money-off vouchers. For distant suppliers keep close tabs on how well they serve your customers.

* Negative feedback is much more likely using dropshipping and other partner companies than where you handle all customer transactions direct. With the wrong partners you could generate bad feeling, requests for refund, negative feedback, dismissal from eBay. Check partner companies by reading feedback from your customers. Look for problem delivery times, product quality concerns,

poor customer service. Mounting negatives with similar complaints signify problems you must correct or seek new suppliers.

* My experience of dropshipping has been exceptionally good. I have companies posting products to my customers minutes after they get my faxed order and they always put my company details into the package, never their own. They don't poach my customers, they've never asked payment from me up front, they're better than I'd hoped for. Getting them was remarkably easy and all down to good communications. I telephone every potential dropshipper before promoting their products. I get to know the other person, determine how serious they are about their business, how approachable they are. Those I have chosen for my business talked more about customers and products than money, they were considerate and caring, keen to please. That first impression has always served me well. Do the same, you won't be disappointed.

* If problems ensue, don't blame the dropshipper without checking first. It could be you haven't explained your requirements properly, they may have serious business or personal problems, it could be coincidence or a batch of particularly difficult customers to blame for those negatives. Be careful,

check thoroughly, and have an emergency plan for major problems. Have plenty of eggs in your basket: use several dropshippers, not just one, and have quality replacements waiting in line.

* Sales materials and graphics are normally provided by larger suppliers or can be downloaded from their web sites. Some have printed catalogues from which you can scan product pictures, others have CDs containing digital pictures. Using their pictures and descriptions makes life a lot easier for you; you won't spend time and money buying products, taking pictures, creating descriptions. But typically, the bigger the company, the more aggressive their marketing, and the more likely their products are known to other eBay sellers. The moral is to not rely solely on these bigger companies. Very often firms without sales materials and graphics are small companies, probably unknown to most other resellers, with fabulous products, and closer control over quality and communications. Of three companies providing my entire dog jewelry stock, two are one man set ups, the other a father and son business.

* Good organizational and communications skills are needed, especially where you sell hundreds of different products from numerous dropshipping and

supplying companies. I've seen PowerSellers listing hundreds of thousands of products at one time, all totally different, and obviously from lots of individual suppliers. Imagine taking just one thousand orders a month (many eBayers take tens of thousands), where you must ensure each order reaches the correct fulfilment company, with accurate customer details, and proper payment. Complicated and very time-consuming! Far better sell a smaller range of high profit items from a few select suppliers.

* Check competition on eBay for your dropshipping company and their products before planning to sell. I found a wonderful dropship firm for CDs, there were hundreds of different titles, their graphics were bright and colorful, a more professional organization was difficult to find.

* Search competition for your product by keying the name, title or maker's name into the search box top right on eBay's home page. No entries for similar products might be good news for you, might because others might still be selling these products, just not right now. Bad news too because others might have tried selling similar products with little success. Lots of entries signals lots of competition, but view listings first to check similarity to your product. Where you find just a few people selling similar products, see

how much they charge, check completed listings for how many sold and how many second chance offers were possible. More than five firms selling similar products worldwide, I'd say is one or two firms too many, except where they sell through auction and you choose shop only listings. If overseas firms sell similar products, but not internationally, consider selling in other countries.

I've covered a bunch of information so far, discussing everything from the fundamentals of dropshipping to the intricacies of picking a niche and running your business. By now, you should have enough of a foundation to confidently get started researching and launching your own dropshipping business. With so much to consider, it's easy to get overwhelmed and lose track of what's really important. That's why I created this list of the crucial elements to success. These are the core "must-do" actions that will make or break your new venture. If you can successfully execute these, you'll be able to get a lot of other things wrong and still have a great chance at success.

1. Add Value

Having a solid plan for how you can add value to your customers is the most crucial success factor. This is important for all businesses, but much more so in the world of dropshipping, where you'll be competing with legions of other "me too" shops carrying similar products. With dropshipping, it's easy to think you're selling customers a product. But successful small merchants understand that it's not only the product they offer they're selling insights, information and solutions. You think you're an ecommerce merchant but you're also in the information business.

If you're struggling to answer this question for a given niche, you may want to consider picking a different market.

The Key Elements of Success

If you're not able to add value through quality information and guidance, the only thing you're left to compete on is price. While this has been a successful strategy for Walmart, it's not going to help you build a successful drop shipping business.

2. Focus on Marketing and SEO

Coming in a close second to adding value as a key success factor is being able to drive traffic to your new site. The #1 problem and frustration new ecommerce merchants face is a lack of traffic to their websites. Too many merchants slave away for months on the perfect site only to launch it to a world that has no idea it exists.

Marketing and driving traffic is absolutely essential to the success of your business and is difficult to outsource well, especially if you have a small budget and are bootstrapping your business. You need to take the personal initiative to develop your own SEO, marketing, outreach and guest posting skills.

This is particularly crucial during the first 6 to 12 months, when no one knows who you are. Following your site launch, you need to dedicate at least 75% of your time on marketing, SEO and traffic generation for at least 4 to 6 months that's right, 4 to 6 months! Once you've established a solid marketing foundation, you can scale back and coast a bit on the work you put in. But early on, it's impossible to place too much emphasis on marketing.

CHAPTER FOUR

CONCLUSION

In Conclusion

This part of the book summarize and add a little knowledge to what has been written in the body of this book.

Basic requirements that you must meet in order to begin working as a dropshipping professional:

1. Choose a product to sell

2. Locate a supplier who will dropship for you

3. Set up an account with the dropshipper

4. Advertise the product for sale (they suggest eBay, but you can use Amazon.com, your own website or a web store)

5. Use an online processor to accept instant payments

6. Order through the dropshipper (your supplier)

7. Follow up after every sale

Think of these things as a good foundation, but also consider the other components. For example, one blogger explains that their dropshipping business uses a web store, supply chain, and good marketing for success. However, it is ill advised to take such advice as you must spend time choosing between suppliers, exploring your options in a well designed web store or site, and planning your marketing and promotions to ensure you are as competitive and profitable as possible.

So, how do you create a successful dropshipping enterprise? You blend those two lists together. Doing so will guarantee you the least stressful setup, planning and launching. In the sections that follow, we are going to look at:

1. Identifying your products

2. Choosing suppliers and building a dependable supply chain

3. Creating your website and/or web store

4. Marketing

These points will provide you with the best way to begin your career as a successful dropshipper.

The Necessary Steps

If you explore what the experts have to say about dropshipping, most agree that selecting your niche and the products to sell can be one of the toughest choices. You already know it is a competitive way of doing business, and that margins can be extremely small. So, what this tells you is that the wiser your choice in products, the better your outcome. Naturally, you can choose the perfect products and create a flawless store, but unless you can market effectively, you won't make many sales. I'm going to consider all of these things as your most necessary steps.

Identifying Your Products

If we take a bit of advice from the professionals, we see that most will tell you to avoid choosing a niche or product based entirely on your personal interests or passions. As one group says: "This is an acceptable strategy if being interested in the product is your primary objective, not necessarily business success. But if your #1 goal is to build a profitable dropshipping site, you'll want to consider setting your personal passions aside when doing market research..." (Shopify) This may change if you find that the products that you love or are passionate about meet the criteria for choosing your niche, but for the most part, your decisions have to based on the following issues. (Note: There is no such thing as the perfect niche or product, but doing the research takes you towards the strongest choices.) To sell successfully, you will need to control pricing as much as possible. You can do this by making your own goods, which then takes you out of dropshipping and is not something I'll cover in this book. Alternately, you can arrange for exclusive prices or make arrangements as a limited distributor. This shrinks the market and gives you a chance at bigger margins. If you cannot make such arrangements, sell at the lowest price possible, but not so low that you put yourself out of business. Rather, differentiate yourself by increasing the value of your product through tactics not related to the price.

For example, don't JUST dropship, but also provide information (free eBooks, web pages with authoritative or appealing content, and so on). Make it a joy to shop through your store, show you are providing buyers with answers to their needs or problems, and build inventory that is complementary. As an example, you think it would be good to sell a high-quality skin care product, and you know there is a market for this, but to guarantee your ongoing success you need to determine how to sell multiple kinds of skin care products. Rather than marketing one product, selling a range of goods applied in various steps throughout the day or as part of a multi-step regimen (i.e. cleansing, toning, moisturizing, etc.)

will ensure a complementary range of goods. Then, you can add value by offering free guides on optimal skin care, and so on.

Products with Increased Value Are Ideal

Some of the basic methods of increasing value without adding to the cost of goods or business include:

Buyer guides

Better and more explanatory product descriptions in perfectly written English

How to or setup guides

Video guides

Comparison tables and guides for the products sold

Use these ideas to help you find your niche, but also keep the intended audience in mind. For example, most dropshipping experts say that repeat buyers, hobbyists and businesses are the best demographics from which to choose your niche. As an example, you might sell natural supplements to fitness centers. This means your clients are the fitness centers, but you also have the individuals using the products as part of the market. Repeat buyers on all fronts! However, if your product is consumable or disposable, you can also ensure that you can build a base of repeat buyers too. This is particularly true when many dropshipping professionals use sites like Amazon.com and its "Subscribe & Save" feature that essentially promises ongoing sales! Also, consider products that have many components or additional items. As an example, cell phones need cases, chargers, screen protectors and more. Most buyers will stay within the same web store when they purchase goods, so always keep those complementary and accessory goods in mind when identifying your niche. You can also steer yourself towards the right products by visualizing how you are going to market them. Is it something you can easily imagine doing? Are there different ways you can see yourself writing or promoting the products? If so, you are probably on the right track. You can also choose a product or niche that is tough to find in your area. It could be almost anything, but if it is hard to get, it will usually have a market.

Choosing Suppliers and Building a Dependable Supply Chain

Supply chain is a term you can use to describe how the goods you sell go from manufacturing to your buyers. Your part in this "chain" is as a service provider as well as a retailer. You are not a manufacturer who creates goods and sells them to wholesalers or retailers. You are not a wholesaler who is going to purchase bulk quantities to sell to retailers, instead you are actually a retailer. You sell to the public at a markup. The big issue to take away from this explanation is that not everyone who says they are a wholesaler actually is one...they could be a retailer selling to you under false terms. In other words, choosing your suppliers and creating a functional supply chain that runs from the manufacturer to your buyers means doing some research. A firm that calls itself a wholesaler or even a dropshipper may be charging too much. As one website warns, "it's critical to know how to differentiate between legitimate wholesale suppliers and retail stores posing as wholesale suppliers. A true wholesaler buys directly from the manufacturer and will usually be able to offer you significantly better pricing."

Since it is your margins that will make or break your business, take the time to recognize the fakers. How? Most will ask you to pay a series of regular "fees" such as a monthly business fee or some sort of ongoing financial obligation. This is completely illegitimate. Another warning sign is any firm that sells directly to the public. This makes them a retailer and not a wholesaler or dropshipper.

You can expect to pay a true dropshipping firm per order fees and you may be required to meet their minimum order sizes. In other words, to create credit with them, you may need to pre-pay for a few hundred dollars worth of product. This is not uncommon, but it may also not be required. How do you find the valid dropshippers or wholesalers? There are a number of paths that can lead you to valid dropshipping and wholesale suppliers:

Use Directories - These are databases of suppliers that are usually arranged by niche or product. Some of the biggest names include Doba, Worldwide Brands, SaleHoo, Wholesale Central, GoGo Dropship Directory, . Note that some of them ask for monthly access fees, and this is not the same as the fees we mentioned above. In this case, you are paying for access to the database, and that is entirely valid.

Directly contact manufacturers - You can locate a legitimate wholesaler easily if you just get in touch with a company to find out who wholesales their goods.

Use the Internet - We now "Google" everything, and you can also use this search engine to find wholesalers. The best way is put your search terms in brackets, i.e. "all natural supplements for weight lifters wholesalers" and then be prepared to dig deep into the search results.

Go to a trade show - Once you know your niche or market, you can easily find trade shows and meet the wholesalers and manufacturers in person. Discuss your needs and ask all of the questions you have, and use this as an ideal opportunity for getting into contact with most of your industry suppliers.

Order from your competitors - If you are struggling to find wholesalers or valid dropshippers, just place an order through one or more of your competitors. The shipping label will have the original shipping address and you can use that to "Google" the name of the company.

Once you have suppliers and can begin to know what you will earn from sales, it is time to begin to create your actual business. In fact, most of the sellers or suppliers will not sell to you unless you are an authentic and legal business entity. These firms are going to be able easily to process your orders, package and ship them, include an invoice and label that features your name and logo, and even handle returns. You will receive the order through the web store, place that order with the supplier and pay them for it, and that is it! First, though, you must create the business and build the online store.

Creating Your Store or Sales Channel

When you are sure that your niche is profitable and that you will be able to market and sell the goods, you can take the next steps forward. This includes choosing the business structure you will use and registering your business name. You must then create a web presence. You can do this in two ways - building a store or site OR using an available web channel.

The most common channels are eBay and Amazon. Both provide you with immediate audiences, nearly instant startup processes, and less need for marketing. Both also have their downsides that include fees, the need to monitor and relist, no customization, no customer relationships, and to hand over your sales data to a company like Amazon. That means you can built your own online store. This gives more control, allows you to customize the look, avoid fees, and create a relationship with customers. In other words, it is more of an authentic business. Because of that, naturally, it is more involved where setup and commitment of time is concerned. Hobbyists tend to use eBay and Amazon while those who are serious about building their business over the long term will create a store or site. Many also end up using all of the sales channels! To build your site, you need to tackle the following:

Setting up a real business

Getting a domain name

Arranging web hosting and setting up the site - this is a big undertaking that includes listing products, using detailed descriptions, arranging for the payment options, dealing with taxes and shipping integration, and so on.

Managing the site

It can be tough to get a business name and web URL or domain name that are a perfect match. However, you want to always choose a domain name that sounds trustworthy and not "fly by night". As a perfect example, consider something like naturalskincare.com (which is a randomly created domain name) versus something like skincreem4u.biz (also randomly created). The first one is more appealing and trustworthy and a good model to use when looking for the domain. In general, choose a domain name that is relevant, simple and short, easy to remember and type, professional and available. How do you get a domain? There are web-hosting services in great abundance. Many provide you with package deals that allow you to register the domain name and provide you with the platform upon which your site is built and kept up and running. While

GoDaddy is one of the biggest names in the world of domain names and hosting, there are many others. HostGator, DreamHost, Hostwinds, Liquid Web, 1&1 Web Hosting, Bluehost, HostMonster and SiteGround are all comparable options, and there are even more to try. Explore user reviews and be sure that they work with WordPress. This is a framework for blogs, web stores, and websites and is removes all of the coding that was once essential for a website to operate. If a web hosting service is designed properly, it will allow you to install WordPress with a single click and provide you with fast speeds and a high percentage of up time (meaning multiple servers that ensure your site is never down or unavailable).

After choosing a domain, getting your web hosting and installing WordPress, you will have to choose a theme. Though you can skip it, your site is going to be far too plain to generate attention and sales. That makes it the time to choose a theme. There are scores of theme providers, some offering free options and some asking for very reasonable rates. The themes you will want to use are those with eCommerce plug ins that allow you to create an online store easily. After you begin to build the site, it is time to consider the details of marketing. This is a bit more involved in the world of online sales, but it can actually be one of the most enjoyable and exciting elements of dropshipping as a career.

Before we move to that, though, one word of wisdom is to consider the use of a multichannel inventory and order management software package or service. Dropshipping is now becoming a tactic that online retailers use to build their portfolio of sales channels. This is a bit more complex than a single dropshipping business. If you are interested in easily managing more than a single sales channel, such as a web store as a dropshipper and a sales page at Amazon or eBay, you may want to explore options for multichannel inventory and order management. One strong example is the Orderhive software that can provide dropshipping support, but also additional features if you are really going to cover multiple channels of sales.

Marketing

As you build your web store, you see that you need product titles and descriptions. You have pages of material to create, and each is an opportunity to market. Additionally, as a business professional with a web presence of any kind (including your eBay or Amazon stores) you can use standard online marketing methods to draw traffic to your pages. The most straightforward methods include:

Social media

Blogging

Email marketing

Videos

Printed material like posters and flyers

PPC ads and banner ads

Partnerships with complementary dropshipping professionals

Hosting or participating in events and shows

Participating in affiliate programs

Word of mouth

Value added material like free eBooks, guides, and that allow you to gather emails or phone numbers for further marketing

SEO

We need to consider that last point in a bit of detail. That is because SEO is the one way to ensure you enjoy online success in your dropshipping endeavors. It is the one sure way to keep traffic headed to your site and is what you will find yourself doing roughly 75% of the time during the first few months you are in business. It is too complicated to teach you to do here, but you will need to spend time learning which keywords are the most potent for your niche, and then use them in everything from page titles and product descriptions to social media posts and your actual web pages.

The best of luck to you in this exciting endeavor!

www.ingramcontent.com/pod-product-compliance
Lightning Source LLC
Chambersburg PA
CBHW071705210326
41597CB00017B/2346